C000186671

CONTENTS

PROLOGUE

A Journey to the Land of Smiles

Welcome, dear reader, to a world where lush green fields meet the horizon, where the warm tropical breeze carries the whispers of a simpler life, and where family values and self-sufficiency are celebrated. You may already be familiar with my family's adventures through our YouTube channel "Life In Bamboo", as we share our experiences of living in rural Thailand. In this book, we invite you to join us on a deeper exploration of our journey, as we seek to inspire and guide those who dream of making Thailand their new home.

Allow me to introduce myself. My name is Ryan, and alongside my loving family, I have embarked on an adventure that has spanned over 15 years in the Land of Smiles. Through our YouTube channel, we have endeavored to promote a self-sufficient lifestyle and to instill the importance of strong family bonds.

Within our little world, I am blessed with two incredible sons, Otis and Hugo, who have grown up embracing the beauty of rural Thailand. Their curiosity and enthusiasm for this enchanting country are a constant reminder of the magic that lies within its borders. Alongside them stands my beloved wife, Damo, a pillar of strength and support in this grand adventure we have chosen.

During my time in Thailand, I have worn many hats, immersing myself in diverse endeavors that have shaped my understanding of this captivating land. From my early days as a teacher, sharing knowledge and exchanging cultural insights, to venturing into entrepreneurship with ventures like my Saxophone Lounge—a haven of smooth jazz and soulful melodies in Hua Hin —I have experienced the vibrant tapestry of Thai life firsthand.

To truly connect with the people and culture, I have dedicated myself to learning the local language. Thai, with its melodious tones and intricate script, has become a bridge that has allowed me to forge meaningful connections and engage in genuine conversations with the wonderful individuals who call this place home.

Throughout the pages of this book, I will draw upon my experiences and insights, offering guidance and practical advice for those who share our dream of calling Thailand their own. From the challenges and triumphs of rural living to the intricacies of navigating Thai society, my aim is to equip you with the knowledge and understanding to embark on your own transformative journey.

So, fasten your seatbelt and prepare to immerse yourself in the tapestry of Thailand. Let the stories, and information within these pages ignite your imagination and embolden your spirit. Together, we will navigate the twists and turns, uncover hidden gems, and unlock the secrets of a life well-lived in the Land of Smiles.

With gratitude and a warm Sawasdee, let our adventure begin.

CHAPTERS

1. INTRODUCTION TO THAI CULTURE AND CUSTOMS

1.1 Overview of Thai Culture: Unveiling the Rich Tapestry

Thai culture is rich and diverse, shaped by its long history, Buddhism, and influences from neighboring countries. Here are some key ways in which it differs from the West:

1. Respect and Politeness: Respect for others is deeply ingrained in Thai culture. Thai people greet each other with a traditional wai, a gesture of respect, and use polite language when addressing others. Respecting elders and those in authority is highly valued.

2. Buddhism: Buddhism is the predominant religion in Thailand, and its teachings have a profound influence on Thai culture. Temples, monks, and Buddhist rituals are an integral part of daily life. Concepts such as karma, merit-making, and the pursuit of inner peace are important in Thai society.

3. Hierarchical Society: Thai society places emphasis on hierarchy and social status. People are expected to show deference to those of higher social standing, such as elders or those in positions of authority. This is reflected in language usage and behavior.

4. Sense of Community: Thais have a strong sense of community and place a high value on social harmony. Family, extended relatives, and close-knit communities play a central role in Thai life. Loyalty and support for one's family and community are highly regarded.

5. Food and Cuisine: Thai cuisine is renowned for its bold flavors, aromatic herbs, and spices. Food holds a special place in Thai culture, often bringing people together. The concept of sharing and communal dining is common, with dishes served in the center of the table for everyone to enjoy.

6. Festivals and Traditions: Thailand is known for its vibrant festivals and traditions. Songkran, the Thai New Year, Loy Krathong, and the Phi Ta Khon Ghost Festival are just a few examples of the colorful celebrations that take place throughout the year.

7. Non-Confrontational Communication: Thai culture values saving face and avoiding confrontation. Directly expressing disagreement or criticism is often avoided, and instead, non-verbal cues, indirect communication, or subtle hints may be used to convey messages.

8. Spirituality and Animism: Alongside Buddhism, animistic beliefs are also prevalent in Thai culture. Many Thais hold beliefs in spirits and supernatural forces, often observing rituals and making offerings to appease them.

9. Land of Smiles: Thailand is often referred to as the "Land of Smiles" due to the friendly and welcoming nature of its people. Smiling is considered a way to show politeness, warmth, and approachability.

It's important to note that culture is complex and diverse, and these points are just a general overview. Thai culture continues to evolve and adapt to modern influences while retaining its unique identity and traditions.

1.2 Cultural Etiquette and Customs: Navigating the Thai Social Landscape

A s you prepare to immerse yourself for Thai society, it's crucial to acquaint yourself with the intricacies of local customs and traditions. Let's unravel the secrets of Thai etiquette together!

Allow me to regale you with a tale that serves as a cautionary reminder for even the most intrepid of adventurers. Imagine our protagonist, let's call him Mark, who decided to partake in a friendly game of Muay Thai—Thailand's traditional martial art. Filled with excitement, Mark entered the ring ready to showcase his skills. Little did he know that in the realm of Muay Thai, one must never touch the head of an opponent, as it is considered highly disrespectful. In the heat of the moment, Mark made an impulsive move and instinctively ruffled his opponent's hair— a gesture of camaraderie in his culture. The crowd fell silent, and an invisible wave of shock rippled through the arena. Mark's well-intentioned action had inadvertently violated a significant cultural taboo, leaving him red-faced and apologetic. I have been there myself on a number of occasions!

Now, let's delve into some essential pointers on Thai etiquette to ensure smooth interactions and avoid any unintended missteps:

1. Respect for Elders: Thai society places great importance on respect for elders. When in the presence of older individuals, be sure to greet them with a wai—the traditional Thai gesture of respect—by pressing your palms together in a prayer-like position and slightly bowing your head. This simple act shows reverence and sets the tone for positive interactions.

2. Saving Face: Thais value harmonious relationships and saving face in social interactions. Avoid confrontational or aggressive behavior, as it can cause embarrassment and loss of face. Instead, strive for diplomacy, compromise, and maintaining a friendly demeanor.

3. Polite Language: Learning a few basic Thai phrases can go a long way in showing respect and fostering connections. Use "khrap" (for males) or "ka" (for females) as a polite ending to your sentences when speaking with locals. For example, "Thank you" would be "Khob khun khrap/ka."

4. Eating Etiquette: When dining with Thais, there are a few customs to keep in mind. It is polite to wait for the eldest or the most senior person to begin eating before you start. Also, refrain from sticking your chopsticks upright in a bowl of rice, as it resembles a ritual performed at funerals.

5. Public Displays of Affection: While Thai society is generally tolerant, it is advisable to exercise discretion when it comes to public displays of affection. Demonstrations of affection such as kissing and hugging are best reserved for private settings.

6. Temples and Monks: When visiting temples, dress modestly and respectfully, covering your shoulders and knees. Remove your shoes before entering temple buildings, and avoid pointing your feet toward Buddha images or monks, as it is considered impolite.

7. Accepting and Offering Gifts: When giving or receiving gifts, use both hands to present or receive them as a sign of respect. Avoid giving items wrapped in white, as it is associated with

funerals. Instead, opt for vibrant colors that symbolize joy and prosperity.

Remember, these etiquette pointers are your key to unlocking the hearts and minds of the Thai people. Embrace the customs, learn from the experiences of others, and let the harmony of Thai society embrace you in return. By practicing these cultural nuances, you'll navigate the social landscape of Thailand with grace and respect. The path to cultural understanding is paved with humorous anecdotes and valuable lessons, ensuring your journey is filled with memorable experiences and genuine connections. So, go forth with an open mind, a respectful heart, and a dash of humor, and discover the beauty of Thai etiquette as it weaves its way into your own remarkable story.

1.3 Festivals and Traditions

From exuberant celebrations to sacred rituals, Thailand is a land where festivities ignite the spirit and bring communities together. If you're eager to immerse yourself in the cultural richness of this country, get ready for a whirlwind of joyous events.

Many of these enchanting festivals have been captured and shared on our YouTube channel, where we've brought the sights, sounds, and vibrant energy of these celebrations to life. So, if you want to dive deeper into the magic of these festivals, be sure to check out our vlogs for a front-row seat to the action.

In the province of Buriram, where we reside, we have the opportunity to experience some unique rural festivals with a distinct Khmer influence. The local communities here have preserved age-old traditions that blend Thai and Khmer customs, creating a captivating cultural fusion.

Here are some key festivals in rural Thailand and their meanings:

- "Poi Sang Long" Ceremony: A rite of passage for young boys of Thai Yai and Khmer heritage, symbolizing their spiritual journey and dedication to Buddhism.

- "Bun Bang Fai" (Rocket Festival): A lively event held during the rainy season to bring rain and fertility to the land, where communities compete to launch homemade rockets into the sky.

- "Bun Khao Phansa" (Candle Festival): Celebrated at the beginning of Buddhist Lent, it marks the start of the rainy season retreat for monks and is accompanied by elaborate candle processions.

- "Yasothon Rocket Festival": Held annually in Yasothon province, this festival showcases massive rockets that soar into the sky in a thrilling competition.

- "Bun Phawet" (Spirit Medium Festival): A fascinating event where spirit mediums channel deities and perform rituals to bring blessings, protection, and healing to the community.

- "Buffalo Racing Festival": Witness the adrenaline-pumping spectacle of buffalo races, where jockeys ride bareback on these magnificent creatures in a thrilling display of skill and speed.

Beyond these local festivals, Thailand boasts a rich tapestry of national celebrations that showcase the country's cultural heritage. From the exuberant water fights of Songkran, where the entire nation comes alive with laughter and splashes, to the breathtaking spectacle of Loy Krathong, where candlelit floats are released onto rivers and lakes, each festival carries its own unique charm and significance.

As you embark on your Thai adventure, keep an eye on the calendar and immerse yourself in the festivities that ignite your curiosity. Engage with the locals, learn the traditional dances, indulge in mouthwatering street food, and let the spirit of celebration fill your heart. Whether you're dancing in the vibrant procession of a rural festival or joining the joyous chaos of a national event, these moments will leave an indelible mark on your journey.

So, let the festivals of Thailand be your guide to the pulsating heart of the culture. Watch our vlogs for a glimpse into the rural festivals of Buriram and the captivating Khmer influence, and let the magic of these traditions weave their spell around you.

1.4 Cuisine

P repare your taste buds for an adventure like no other. Whether you're a culinary enthusiast or simply appreciate good food, Thailand offers a tantalizing array of flavors and dishes that will leave you craving for more.

One of the advantages of living in rural Thailand is the significant difference in cost compared to the bustling cities. While you may find that dining in the cities can be a bit pricier, exploring the local food scene in rural areas is a delightful and budget-friendly experience. In fact, you'll be pleasantly surprised by the affordability of delicious meals that can be found in humble street stalls, local markets, and small family-run restaurants.

For example, a steaming bowl of fragrant and flavorful Thai noodle soup, such as "boat noodles" or "kuay teow," can be savored for as little as 30 to 50 baht. These noodle delights are often accompanied by tender slices of beef, meatballs, or succulent pork, swimming in a rich broth that will warm your soul.

When it comes to homemade meals, nothing can beat the culinary prowess of my wife's mother, Yai. Her home-cooked dishes are truly a masterpiece, crafted with love and generations of culinary wisdom. I must confess, her cooking is the best I've ever had. From spicy stir-fries bursting with fresh herbs and vegetables to aromatic curries that transport you to flavor paradise, every bite is a celebration of taste.

While eating out is generally more affordable in Thailand, especially when indulging in local cuisine, you may find that cooking Western dishes at home can be a bit pricier due to the higher cost of imported ingredients. However, fear not! Thailand offers a wide range of markets and grocery stores where you can find most of the essentials. And for those hard-to-find items from your home country, online platforms like Lazada come to the rescue, delivering a taste of familiarity right to your doorstep.

Now, I must confess, I'm not what you would call a "foodie." Our YouTube channel doesn't often feature food, but when it does, it's truly a gastronomic adventure worth savoring. From exploring hidden local eateries tucked away in bustling markets to indulging in unique regional specialties, we've discovered some hidden culinary gems that have left us in awe. So, keep an eye out for those rare food-focused episodes, as they offer a mouthwatering glimpse into the diverse and delectable world of Thai cuisine.

Whether you're delighting in the exquisite simplicity of street food or savoring the home-cooked delights of Yai's kitchen, let the tantalizing aromas and vibrant flavors awaken your senses. And remember, in Thailand, good food is not just a meal—it's a celebration of life itself.

1.5 Religion and Spirituality

I n the land of temples and serene spirituality, religion holds a special place in the hearts of many Thais. Buddhism, the predominant religion in Thailand, weaves its way into the fabric of everyday life, shaping beliefs, traditions, and the way people interact with the world around them.

At the heart of Buddhism lie the Four Noble Truths, which teach that life is inherently characterized by suffering, but there is a path to liberation from this suffering. The Eightfold Path, a guiding principle for leading a righteous and fulfilling life, encompasses virtues such as right understanding, right intention, right speech, right action, right livelihood, right effort, right mindfulness, and right concentration.

In rural areas of Thailand, such as where we live in Buriram, the influence of Khmer culture is also evident. The fusion of Khmer and Thai traditions gives rise to a unique blend of beliefs and practices. Ancient temples adorned with intricate carvings stand as testaments to this rich historical heritage.

Now, when it comes to my personal beliefs, I find myself drawn to a blend of Buddhist and Hindu philosophies. The reverence for nature, karma, and the interconnectedness of all beings resonates deeply within me. It's this amalgamation of beliefs that shapes my perspective and understanding of the world.

What makes Thailand truly remarkable is its inclusiveness and acceptance of diverse beliefs. Whether one follows Buddhism, Islam, Christianity, Hinduism, or any other faith, the Thai people greet them with open hearts and warm smiles. This spirit of tolerance and respect is one of the cornerstones of Thai society, fostering harmony and unity among its people.

In terms of data, it's important to note that approximately

95% of Thais identify as Buddhists, while Islam, Christianity, and Hinduism make up the religious minority. The presence of various religious communities creates a vibrant tapestry of faith and spirituality, adding to the cultural richness of Thailand.

As you embark on your journey through the spiritual landscapes of Thailand, immerse yourself in the tranquility of sacred temples, engage in meaningful conversations with local monks, and embrace the inclusive and accepting nature of this remarkable country. Whether you seek solace, seek answers, or seek enlightenment, Thailand offers a sanctuary where all paths are welcomed and respected.

2. EXPLORING LIVING OPTIONS IN THAILAND

2.1: Contrasting City Living and Rural Life in Thailand

I n this chapter, we'll explore the stark differences between city living and the serenity of rural life in Thailand. As someone who has experienced both, I can provide insights and practical advice to help you make an informed decision about where to call home.

2.1.1 Finding Accommodation: City Vs. Rural

When it comes to finding accommodation, the approach differs depending on whether you're seeking the bustling energy of city life or the tranquil seclusion of rural areas. In my experience, the best way to find affordable housing is by embarking on your own adventure. Hop on a motorbike and explore the neighborhoods, keeping an eye out for "For Rent" signs. Often, you'll stumble upon hidden gems that aren't listed online or through agents. It's a delightful way to immerse yourself in the local community and discover unique rental opportunities.

For those considering more expensive of specialist properties, utilizing real estate agents is a more common practice. They have access to a wide range of properties and can guide you through the rental process. Be prepared, though, as rents in cities like Bangkok can be much higher compared to rural areas. It's advisable to rent initially, allowing you to experience the neighborhood, gauge the convenience of amenities, and determine if it aligns with your lifestyle before committing to a long-term investment.

2.1.2 Comparing Rental Prices: Urban Centers And Rural Bliss

Let's delve into the numbers and compare rental prices between urban centers and rural areas. In Bangkok, the cost of living can be significantly higher, especially in sought-after neighborhoods and central business districts. Condos and apartments in prime locations may command higher rental fees due to their proximity to amenities and transportation hubs.

In rural areas, the rental landscape is often more affordable. It's not uncommon to find rentals at a fraction of the cost compared to their city counterparts. This affordability can provide you with more financial flexibility to pursue other passions and experiences while enjoying the tranquility and simplicity of rural life, but finding work or building a business in these area is more difficult due to lack of tourists.

On average, a one-bedroom apartment in the heart of Bangkok can range from 15,000 to 100,000 baht per month, depending on the location and amenities. Contrast this with a similar-sized rental in rural areas, which could be as low as 5,000 to 30,000 baht per month, presenting a substantial difference in terms of cost.

It's important to note that rental prices can vary greatly depending on the specific location and the level of development in rural areas. Some areas may have seen increased investment and tourism, leading to slightly higher rental rates. Researching local market trends and seeking advice from locals or expat communities in the area can help you gain a more accurate understanding of rental prices in your desired rural location.

2.1.3 City Buzz Vs. Rural Tranquility: Personal Experiences

Allow me to share my personal experiences of city living versus the peaceful embrace of rural life. Living in the heart of Bangkok, I was surrounded by a constant flurry of activity, bustling streets, and the hum of urban life. The city's vibrancy, endless entertainment options, and convenient access to amenities were undoubtedly appealing. However, I found myself longing for a slower pace, a deeper connection with nature, and a sense of tranquility that eluded me in the urban sprawl.

Making the move to rural Thailand was a transformative experience. The solitude and serenity of waking up to the sounds of nature, the gentle rustling of leaves, and the absence of city noise provided a profound sense of peace. The strong sense of community, the warm smiles of neighbors, and and the slower rhythm of life became the cornerstones of my rural existence. I found myself immersed in the beauty of the countryside, surrounded by verdant fields and the simplicity of everyday life.

While city living offered a myriad of entertainment options, I discovered that rural life had its own unique charms. Instead of bustling nightlife, I embraced the tranquility of stargazing on a clear night, the soothing melodies of birdsong during morning walks, and the simple joy of watching the sunset paint the sky in hues of orange and pink.

One aspect that I particularly cherish about rural living is the genuine warmth and hospitality of the local community. Neighbors become friends, and the sense of belonging is palpable. I found myself engaging in meaningful conversations, participating in local festivities, and experiencing the rich cultural heritage of rural Thailand, influenced by its Khmer roots.

Of course, personal preferences play a significant role in choosing between city living and rural bliss. Some individuals thrive on the energy and diversity of city life, while others seek solace in the tranquility and connection with nature that rural areas provide. It's a matter of finding the right balance that aligns with your values, priorities, and desired lifestyle.

In conclusion, whether you gravitate towards the vibrant pulse of city living or the serenity of rural life, Thailand offers a diverse range of options to suit your preferences. Understanding the contrasting dynamics, rental prices, and personal experiences can help you make an informed decision. Remember, what matters most is finding a place that resonates with your heart, a place you can call home.

2.2 Pros And Cons Of City Living And Rural Life

When considering whether to embrace the energy of city living or the tranquility of rural life in Thailand, it's important to weigh the pros and cons of each. Let's explore some key aspects to help you make an informed decision:

City Living:

Pros:

- Vibrant Lifestyle: Cities like Bangkok offer a dynamic and cosmopolitan lifestyle, with a plethora of entertainment options, shopping malls, restaurants, and cultural events. The city buzzes with activity, ensuring there's always something to do.

- Job Opportunities: Urban centers provide a broader range of job opportunities across various industries, including finance, technology, hospitality, and international business. The competitive job market can offer higher salaries and career growth. I will cover the difficulties with working in a later chapter.

- International Connections: Cities attract a diverse population, fostering a multicultural environment and providing opportunities to connect with people from around the world. Expanding your network and embracing cultural diversity are significant advantages of city living.

- Modern Infrastructure: Urban areas boast modern infrastructure, including efficient public transportation systems, well-equipped healthcare facilities, and a wide range of amenities. Convenience and accessibility are key benefits of city living.

Cons:

- High Costs: City living often comes with higher costs of living, including accommodation, transportation, dining out, and entertainment. Rental prices, especially in prime locations, can be substantially higher compared to rural areas. Daily expenses may require careful budgeting.

- Pollution and Congestion: Urban centers tend to have higher levels of pollution and traffic congestion. Air pollution, noise pollution, and crowded streets are common challenges. However, efforts are being made to improve environmental sustainability in cities.

- Competitive Lifestyle: The fast-paced, competitive nature of city living can be demanding and stressful. The constant hustle and bustle may not suit everyone's temperament. It's important to find a balance and prioritize self-care in a city environment.

Rural Life:

Pros:

- Tranquility and Serenity: Rural areas offer a peaceful escape from the chaos of city life. The natural beauty, fresh air, and open spaces create an environment conducive to relaxation, reflection, and a slower pace of life.

- Lower Cost of Living: One of the major advantages of rural living is the lower cost of living. Housing, daily expenses, and even land prices tend to be more affordable compared to urban areas. This can provide financial freedom and flexibility.

- Community Spirit: Rural communities often have a strong sense of community and neighborly support. People tend to know each other, fostering a warm and welcoming atmosphere. Building connections and forming relationships is often easier in rural areas.

- Closer to Nature: Living in rural areas allows for a deeper connection with nature. Access to outdoor activities such as hiking, biking, and exploring natural landscapes is readily available. It offers an opportunity to appreciate the beauty and tranquility of Thailand's countryside.

Cons:

- Limited Amenities: Rural areas may have limited access to certain amenities and services. Shopping malls, specialized healthcare facilities, and entertainment options might require traveling to nearby towns or cities.

- Job Opportunities: While some rural areas have emerging industries and job prospects, the range of employment opportunities may be more limited compared to urban centers. Remote work or self-employment options can be viable alternatives. I will cover the difficulties with working in a later chapter.

- Education: If you have children, consider the availability and quality of schools in rural areas. Some may have limited options or may require longer commutes to access quality education. However, some rural schools offer a more personalized and community-oriented approach to education.

It's crucial to consider your personal preferences, lifestyle, and priorities when weighing the pros and cons of city living and rural life in Thailand. Each

3. NAVIGATING THAI VISA AND IMMIGRATION

3.1 Exploring Visa Options: Which Visa is Right for You?

When planning to live in Thailand, it's crucial to understand the various visa options available and choose the one that suits your circumstances best. Thailand offers different types of visas, each designed for specific purposes and durations of stay. Let's explore some common visa options:

1. Tourist Visa:

- Best Suited for: Those planning a short-term visit or exploring Thailand as a tourist.
- Duration: Typically valid for 60 days, with a possible extension of an additional 30 days.
- Note: The tourist visa is not suitable for long-term stays or

employment.

2. Non-Immigrant Visa:

- Best Suited for: Individuals seeking long-term stay for various purposes, such as employment, business, or education.
- Duration: Varies depending on the specific purpose of the visa and the supporting documentation.
- Note: Non-Immigrant visas require specific requirements and documentation based on the purpose of stay.

A. Non-Immigrant O Visa (Marriage):

- Best Suited for: Individuals married to Thai citizens or permanent residents of Thailand.
- Financial Requirement: Applicants are required to show a minimum of 400,000 Thai Baht in a Thai bank account or a monthly income of at least 40,000 Thai Baht. Alternatively, a combination of both savings and income can be demonstrated.
- Duration: Initially granted for 90 days, and can be extended for 1 year based on marriage registration and other requirements.
- Note: Non-Immigrant O visas require proof of a genuine relationship with a Thai spouse, including marriage certificates and other supporting documents.

B. Non-Immigrant O-A Visa (Retirement Visa):

- Best Suited for: Retirees aged 50 years or older.
- Financial Requirement: Applicants must have a minimum of 800,000 Thai Baht in a Thai bank account or a monthly income of at least 65,000 Thai Baht. Alternatively, a combination of both savings and income can be demonstrated.

- Duration: Initially granted for 1 year, and can be extended on an annual basis.

- Note: Retirement visas require proof of age and financial stability, along with other supporting documentation.

There are other visas available such as education visa for those wishing to study Thai, Muay Thai or similar here. There is also the Elite visa in which you pay upfront for a number of years in the country. There are indeed a whole host of other visas but the main ones that I would consider for a long term retired or married expat are the above.

In my personal experience, I have held both business visas when I had my businesses in Thailand and currently hold a marriage visa as I am married to a Thai citizen. Each visa has its own requirements and benefits, allowing individuals to stay and engage in activities within the legal framework of the country.

It's important to consult with the Thai immigration authorities or seek advice from professional immigration consultants to ensure you understand the specific requirements, procedures, and limitations associated with each visa type. Immigration laws and regulations may change, so staying informed and complying with the latest guidelines is essential for a smooth and legal stay in Thailand.

Remember, choosing the right visa depends on your specific situation and intentions in Thailand. Take the time to research and assess the visa options available to make an informed decision that aligns with your long-term plans and goals.

3.2 Navigating the Visa Application Process

Obtaining a visa for long-term stay in Thailand requires following specific procedures and submitting the necessary documentation. While some individuals may choose to use immigration agents to assist with their visa applications, my personal preference is to handle the process myself. This allows me to have a clear understanding of the requirements, ensure transparency, and maintain control over the long-term legality of my stay.

Here's an overview of the visa application process in Thailand:

1. Gather Required Documents:

   - Review the specific requirements for your chosen visa type. This may include items such as passport copies, application forms, photographs, proof of funds, marriage certificates (if applicable), and other supporting documents.

2. Prepare Financial Documentation:

   - Depending on the visa type, you will need to demonstrate your financial stability. This may involve showing bank statements, income proof, or a combination of both. It's important to meet the financial requirements specified by the Thai immigration authorities.

3. Complete Application Forms:

   - Fill out the required application forms accurately and thoroughly. Ensure that all information provided is correct and matches the supporting documents.

4. Submit Application:

- Visit the local Thai immigration office or embassy/consulate in your home country to submit your application. Present all required documents and pay the necessary fees. It's advisable to check the specific office's operating hours and any appointment requirements in advance.

5. Attend Visa Interview (If Required):

- Depending on the visa type, you may be called for an interview to further assess your application. Be prepared to answer questions related to your purpose of stay, financial stability, and other relevant details.

6. Visa Processing:

- The processing time varies depending on the visa type and the workload of the immigration office. It's important to allow sufficient time for processing and plan your stay accordingly.

7. Receive Visa:

- Once your application is approved, you will receive your visa. Check the validity and conditions of your visa, including any restrictions or limitations.

By personally handling the visa application process, my wife and I have peace of mind knowing that we have provided accurate information and met all the requirements. We believe that taking responsibility for our own applications reduces the risk of future complications and ensures the long-term legality of our stay in

Thailand.

While immigration agents can be knowledgeable and helpful, it's important to consider the long-term implications and potential risks involved. There have been cases where reliance on agents has led to problems if the financial requirements were not actually met or if incorrect information was provided.

By taking charge of the visa application process ourselves, we maintain control and stay fully accountable for meeting the necessary criteria. We believe it's essential to be informed, follow the correct procedures, and comply with the immigration laws and regulations to ensure a smooth and trouble-free stay in Thailand.

Remember, the visa application process can be complex and requirements may vary depending on the visa type and individual circumstances. It's advisable to consult official sources, such as the Thai immigration authorities or reliable government websites, for the most up-to-date information and guidelines.

3.3 Extending Your Stay in Thailand

I f you've fallen in love with the beauty and charm of Thailand and wish to extend your stay beyond the initial visa period, there are options available to make it happen. Extending your stay in Thailand requires careful planning and adherence to the country's immigration regulations. Here's what you need to know:

1. Visa Extensions:

- Depending on the type of visa you initially entered Thailand with, you may be eligible for a visa extension. The most common visa types for extensions include the Tourist Visa (TR) and the Non-Immigrant Visa (such as the Non-Immigrant B Visa for work or the Non-Immigrant O Visa for retirement or family-related reasons). You can apply for a visa extension at the local immigration office in Thailand.

2. Required Documents:

- When applying for a visa extension, you'll typically need to provide the following documents:
    - Passport: Ensure your passport is valid for at least six months.
    - Departure Card: The departure card given to you upon arrival in Thailand.
    - Completed Application Form: Fill out the required application form for the visa extension.
    - Proof of Financial Means: Depending on the visa type, you may need to show proof of sufficient funds in a Thai bank account or an income affidavit.
    - Supporting Documents: Provide any additional documents required based on your specific visa type.

3. Application Process:

- It's recommended to visit the immigration office well before your current visa expires to allow ample time for processing. Submit your application along with the required documents and pay the applicable fees. The immigration officer will review your application, and if approved, you'll receive an extended stay permit.

4. Overstay Penalties:

- It's essential to adhere to the terms of your visa and avoid overstaying in Thailand. Overstaying beyond the authorized period can result in penalties, fines, or even being barred from re-entering the country. If you realize you've overstayed, it's advisable to rectify the situation by paying the necessary fines and extending your visa as soon as possible.

5. Consult With Immigration Experts:

- If you're unsure about the visa extension process or have complex circumstances, it's wise to seek advice from immigration experts or lawyers who specialize in Thai immigration law. They can provide guidance, assist with the application process, and ensure you comply with all legal requirements.

Extending your stay in Thailand allows you to continue enjoying the beauty, culture, and warmth of this remarkable country. By familiarizing yourself with the visa extension process and staying updated on immigration regulations, you can prolong your stay and create lasting memories in the Land of Smiles.

3.4 Applying for Residency:
Challenges and Considerations

While residing in Thailand long-term can be an enticing prospect, obtaining permanent residency, also known as Thai citizenship, is a complex and challenging process. As an expat who has not yet applied for residency, I understand the difficulties involved. Here are some key points to consider:

1. Eligibility Criteria:

- The criteria for obtaining permanent residency in Thailand are stringent and subject to change. Generally, applicants need to meet specific requirements, including residing in Thailand for a minimum number of years, holding a valid non-immigrant visa, having a clean criminal record, and meeting financial and medical prerequisites. It's important to note that meeting the criteria in the past does not guarantee approval in the present.

2. Limited Number Of Approvals:

- Thailand has a limited quota for granting permanent residency each year. This means that even if you meet all the eligibility criteria, there is no guarantee of being approved. The limited number of approvals can make the process highly competitive and challenging.

3. Documentation And Application Process:

- Applying for residency involves a comprehensive documentation process. This typically includes gathering various supporting documents, such as personal identification, proof of residency, financial statements, tax records, health certificates, and more. The application process can be time-consuming and requires careful attention to detail.

4. Language And Cultural Knowledge:

- Thai language proficiency and knowledge of Thai culture and customs are often assessed during the residency application process. Demonstrating your understanding and appreciation of Thai culture can strengthen your application. However, language and cultural barriers can pose challenges for some applicants.

5. Legal And Professional Assistance:

- Due to the complexities involved, seeking legal or professional assistance from immigration experts or lawyers who specialize in Thai residency matters can be beneficial. They can guide you through the process, ensure all required documents are in order, and provide invaluable advice based on their expertise and experience.

It's essential to weigh the benefits and challenges of applying for residency in Thailand. While permanent residency offers certain advantages, such as unrestricted stay and work rights, it requires significant commitment, adherence to legal requirements, and patience due to the competitive nature of the process.

As someone who has not applied for residency myself, I understand the complexities and considerations involved. It's important to stay updated on the latest regulations, consult with professionals, and make an informed decision based on your specific circumstances and long-term plans in Thailand.

And remember, while obtaining permanent residency in Thailand can be challenging, it's not the only path to enjoying a fulfilling and enriching life in the country. Many expats choose to live in Thailand on long-term visas or through the renewal of non-immigrant visas, such as marriage visas or business visas. These options provide flexibility and allow you to enjoy the benefits of living in Thailand without pursuing permanent residency.

Ultimately, the decision to apply for residency should be based on your individual circumstances, goals, and long-term plans. It's advisable to carefully evaluate the requirements, seek professional advice if needed, and consider the potential challenges and benefits before embarking on the residency application process.

Remember, Thailand offers a warm and welcoming environment to expats, and whether you choose to pursue permanent residency or not, you can still enjoy the vibrant culture, friendly communities, and incredible experiences that the country has to offer.

4. ESSENTIAL SERVICES AND UTILITIES

4.1: Healthcare and Medical Services in Thailand

I n this chapter, we'll delve into the healthcare system and medical services available in Thailand. It's crucial to have access to quality healthcare when living in a new country, and Thailand is renowned for its affordable and reliable medical facilities.

4.1.1 Public Healthcare System

Thailand has a robust public healthcare system that provides accessible and affordable medical services to its citizens and expatriates. The Ministry of Public Health oversees the public healthcare system, which includes government-run hospitals, clinics, and health centers throughout the country. These facilities offer a range of medical services, from primary care to specialized treatments, at significantly lower costs compared to many other countries.

Expats residing in Thailand can also avail themselves of the public healthcare system. It's important to note that while the quality of care in public hospitals is generally good, there may be language barriers and longer waiting times due to the high patient volume in cities. However, for routine check-ups, minor illnesses, and emergencies, public healthcare facilities can be a cost-effective and reliable option.

4.1.2 Private Healthcare And International Hospitals

Thailand is well-known for its private healthcare sector, which offers world-class medical services and facilities. Private hospitals in major cities like Bangkok, Chiang Mai, and Phuket cater to both local and international patients, providing a higher standard of care, shorter waiting times, and English-speaking staff.

International hospitals in Thailand are particularly popular among expats and tourists. These hospitals are equipped with state-of-the-art technology, internationally trained doctors, and a comprehensive range of medical specialties. From general consultations to specialized surgeries, these hospitals offer a wide array of medical services, including dental care, cosmetic procedures, and wellness treatments.

It's important to note that private healthcare services come at a higher cost compared to public facilities. Expats are advised to have health insurance coverage that includes private hospital care to mitigate potential expenses.

4.1.3 Health Insurance

Having comprehensive health insurance is crucial when living in Thailand. This could be one of your biggest costs depending on your age, but it provides financial protection and ensures access to quality healthcare services. There are various health insurance options available, including local and international insurance providers. It's essential to carefully review and compare policies to determine the coverage that best suits your needs.

When selecting health insurance, consider factors such as coverage for inpatient and outpatient services, emergency medical care, prescription medications, and specialized treatments. It's also important to check whether the insurance covers both public and private hospitals, as well as the network of healthcare providers available.

4.1.4 Medical Tourism

Thailand has gained a reputation as a global hub for medical tourism. Many people travel to Thailand specifically for medical treatments and procedures due to the country's high-quality healthcare services, affordability, and renowned expertise in certain medical fields such as cosmetic surgery, dental care, and fertility treatments.

Medical tourists benefit from the combination of top-notch medical care, state-of-the-art facilities, and the opportunity to recover in a beautiful and culturally rich destination. However, it's important to conduct thorough research, choose reputable hospitals and clinics, and consult with medical professionals before undergoing any treatments or procedures.

4.2: Education in Thailand

E ducation is a crucial consideration when moving to a new country, and Thailand offers a variety of schooling options to meet the needs of different families.

4.2.1 Public Schools

Thailand has a comprehensive public school system that provides education to Thai nationals. Public schools follow the Thai curriculum and primarily use the Thai language for instruction. While public schools are an option for expat children, the language barrier and cultural differences can pose challenges for non-Thai speakers.

4.2.2 International Schools

International schools are a popular choice for expat families in Thailand. These schools offer an international curriculum, often based on British, American, or International Baccalaureate (IB) standards. They provide instruction in English and offer a multicultural learning environment that caters to the needs of expatriate students.

International schools in Thailand vary in terms of size, facilities, and fees. Larger cities like Bangkok, Chiang Mai, and Phuket have a wide range of international schools to choose from. On average, annual tuition fees for international schools in Thailand can range from 400,000 to 1,200,000 baht, depending on the school's reputation, facilities, and curriculum.

4.2.3 Homeschooling

Homeschooling is another option for expat families in Thailand. Some families choose to educate their children at home to provide a more personalized and flexible learning experience. This approach allows for tailored curricula, individualized attention, and the ability to incorporate a child's interests and learning style into their education.

If you're considering homeschooling, it's important to familiarize yourself with the legal requirements and regulations in Thailand. The Ministry of Education sets guidelines for homeschooling, including curriculum standards and reporting obligations. Engaging with local homeschooling communities and seeking guidance from experienced homeschooling parents can provide valuable insights and support.

4.2.4 Local Private Schools

Local private schools can be an affordable option for expat families seeking a blend of local culture and education. These schools often provide instruction in both Thai and English, offering a balanced approach to language development. While the majority of subjects are taught in Thai, many private schools dedicate specific hours for English language instruction.

In our case, homeschooling our son Otis for the first five years and transitioning him to a local private school was a unique path. This allowed us to provide individualized education while integrating him into the local community. The private school's focus on English language instruction for one hour each day aligns with our goal of nurturing his bilingual abilities. The average tuition fees for local private schools in Thailand can range from 20,000 to 50,000 baht per term, depending on the school's location and facilities.

Remember, when selecting an educational option for your child, consider factors such as curriculum, language of instruction, teaching methodologies, extracurricular activities, and the overall learning environment. It's important to find a school that supports your child's academic and personal growth while fostering a sense of belonging and cultural integration.

Thailand offers a diverse range of educational opportunities for expat families. Whether you choose public schools, international schools, homeschooling, or local private schools,it's crucial to consider your child's needs, language abilities, and educational goals to make an informed decision.

4.3: Banking and Financial Matters

Managing your finances effectively is an important aspect of living abroad, and Thailand offers a range of banking services to meet your needs.

4.3.1 Opening A Bank Account

Opening a bank account in Thailand is a straightforward process, especially if you hold a valid work permit. As an expat who has banked with SCB for most of my time here, I was able to open my account using my work permit. Opening a bank account in Thailand can be done even if you don't have a valid work permit.

While requirements may vary from bank to bank, the following general guidelines can give you an idea of the process:

1. Choose a Bank: Research and select a reputable bank in Thailand that suits your needs. Popular options for expats include Bangkok Bank, Kasikorn Bank, and SCB.

2. Required Documents: Prepare the necessary documents, which typically include:

   - Passport: Provide a valid passport with a non-immigrant visa or tourist visa.
   - Proof of Address: Present a utility bill or rental agreement showing your current address in Thailand.

3. Initial Deposit: Be prepared to make an initial deposit into your new bank account. The required amount may vary depending on the bank and the type of account you choose.

4. Application Process: Visit the bank branch in person to complete the application process. Fill out the necessary forms and provide the required documents. The bank staff will guide you through the process and assist with any questions you may have.

5. Verification and Approval: The bank will review your application and documents for verification. This process may take a few days to complete. Once approved, you will receive your bank account details, including your account number and any associated debit or ATM cards.

By following these steps, you can open a bank account in Thailand and gain access to the banking services and facilities offered by reputable institutions. Having a local bank account can simplify your financial transactions, enable electronic transfers, and provide a secure place to store your funds while living in Thailand as an expat.

It's important to note that specific requirements may vary from bank to bank, so it's advisable to inquire directly with the bank you wish to open an account with. Some companies offer services to open an account for you such as Siam Legal in Thailand.

4.3.2 Online Banking And Mobile Apps

Thai banks, including SCB, have embraced technology, providing convenient online banking services and mobile apps. These digital platforms offer a wide range of functionalities, including fund transfers, bill payments, balance inquiries, and account management. The ease of use and accessibility of these apps make it convenient for you to manage your finances on the go, whether you're in Thailand or abroad.

4.3.3 Money Transfers

Transferring money between your home country and Thailand is a common need for expats. Using services like TransferWise, now called "Wise," can be a great choice for international money transfers. Wise offers competitive exchange rates and low fees, allowing you to transfer money quickly and securely. Their user-friendly platform makes it easy to initiate transfers and track the progress of your transactions.

My link is: https://wise.com/invite/inh/ryank559

4.3.4 Currency Exchange And Atms

Thailand is well-equipped with currency exchange services and ATMs, making it easy for expats to access cash and convert currencies. ATMs are widely available throughout the country, and most accept international debit and credit cards. However, it's important to be aware of any fees or charges that may apply when using ATMs abroad. You can also visit authorized currency exchange counters, which are commonly found in airports, shopping malls, and tourist areas, to exchange your currency. The rates are high and thats why I use Wise.

4.4: Internet and Communication

Staying connected is essential for many expats, whether it's for work, keeping in touch with loved ones, or simply enjoying online activities.

4.4.1 Internet Infrastructure In Thailand

Thailand has made significant advancements in its internet infrastructure in recent years. Major cities, including Bangkok and other urban centers, offer robust and reliable internet connectivity. High-speed broadband and fiber-optic networks are readily available, providing fast and stable internet connections.

Even in rural areas like Buriram, where I reside on my farm, there has been a remarkable development in internet connectivity. Thanks to the expansion of infrastructure, we now have access to fast 5G internet, allowing us to enjoy high-speed internet for various purposes.

4.4.2 Internet Service Providers

In Thailand, several internet service providers (ISPs) offer a range of plans and packages to cater to different needs and budgets. Some popular ISPs include True Internet, AIS Fibre, and 3BB. These providers offer various internet speed options, allowing you to choose a plan that suits your requirements.

When selecting an ISP, consider factors such as reliability, customer service, and coverage in your specific area. It's worth checking with neighbors or local expat communities to gather recommendations and insights regarding the best ISP options in your locality.

4.4.3 Mobile Networks And Communication

Thailand boasts a well-developed mobile network infrastructure, providing extensive coverage throughout the country. Major mobile network operators include AIS, DTAC, and TrueMove H. These providers offer prepaid and postpaid SIM card options, allowing you to choose a plan that aligns with your communication needs. I usually pay for the internet by the year on DTAC to save big and not have to worry about it.

For expats, obtaining a local SIM card is relatively straightforward. You can visit the nearest mobile network provider's store or purchase SIM cards from convenience stores, malls, or even at the airport upon arrival. Ensure you have your passport with you as it's a requirement for SIM card registration.

With a Thai SIM card, you'll have access to affordable call and data plans, enabling you to stay connected while on the go. It's important to note that different providers may offer varying network coverage, so it's advisable to check the coverage maps or inquire with locals regarding the reliability of mobile networks in your specific area.

By leveraging Thailand's advanced internet infrastructure and mobile networks, you can enjoy seamless communication and stay connected with the world around you, whether you're living in a bustling city or a serene rural setting.

4.5: Utilities and Living Expenses

M anaging your monthly bills is an essential aspect of expat life, and understanding the costs associated with basic amenities can help you plan your budget effectively.

4.5.1 Electricity Costs

Thailand's electricity rates are relatively affordable, especially when compared to some Western countries. The cost of electricity will depend on your usage and the size of your home. In my experience, with an air conditioning unit in the bedroom and average electricity consumption, our monthly electricity bill amounts to less than 5,000 baht.

Additionally, we have invested in an on-grid solar system that helps reduce our electricity costs further. This sustainable solution harnesses the power of the sun and allows us to generate clean energy while minimizing our reliance on the grid. It's a win-win situation for both our budget and the environment.

4.5.2 Internet Expenses

As mentioned earlier, Thailand offers a wide range of internet service providers (ISPs) with various plans and packages. The monthly cost of internet service will depend on the speed and plan you choose. On average, a high-speed internet plan can range from 500 to 1,000 baht per month.

Considering the importance of internet connectivity in our modern lives, investing in a reliable and fast internet plan is a worthwhile decision. With our monthly expenses, including internet and electricity combined, totaling less than 5,000 baht, we can comfortably enjoy the benefits of technology without straining our budget.

4.5.3 Water Supply

In rural areas like Buriram, where we live, water supply can sometimes differ from urban areas. Many rural properties rely on wells for water, which can provide a sustainable and cost-effective solution. We pump water from a well on our property, ensuring a constant supply for daily needs such as cooking, cleaning, and bathing.

Depending on your location, access to clean and reliable water may vary. We always use bottled, but brush our teeth with the well water. It is advisable to always drink from bottled however. It's essential to ensure that your property has a suitable water source, whether it's through a well, a connection to the local water supply, or other means. This will contribute to a smooth and hassle-free living experience.

By keeping your utility bills, including electricity and internet, within a reasonable range and utilizing sustainable solutions like solar power, you can further reduce your living expenses while promoting a greener lifestyle.

5. FINDING ACCOMMODATION IN THAILAND

5.1: Renting vs. Buying Property in Thailand

As an expat who has experienced both renting and the temptation to buy, I can provide insights and cautionary advice to help you make an informed decision.

5.1.1 Renting In Thailand

Renting a property in Thailand offers flexibility, especially for expats who may have uncertain plans or frequently move due to work or personal reasons. The rental market in Thailand is diverse, with options ranging from apartments and condos to townhouses and villas. The availability of rental properties varies depending on the location, and there are numerous attractive areas to choose from.

In popular cities like Bangkok, the average monthly rent for a one-bedroom apartment in the city center can range from 15,000 to 40,000 baht, depending on the location, amenities, and size. In comparison, rental prices in rural areas can be significantly lower, with one-bedroom rentals starting as low as 5,000 to 15,000 baht per month.

5.1.2 Advantages Of Renting

Renting provides several advantages, particularly for expats who are still acclimating to the country or have temporary living arrangements. Here are some key benefits to consider:

1. Flexibility: Renting allows you to be more flexible with your living situation. Whether you're testing out different neighborhoods or adjusting to changes in your personal or professional life, renting gives you the freedom to move without the commitment of long-term ownership.

2. Cost-effective: Renting can be a more affordable option, especially if you're not planning to stay in Thailand for an extended period. Rental costs often pale in comparison to the expenses associated with purchasing property, such as down payments, property taxes, and maintenance fees.

3. Easy maintenance: As a renter, you can often rely on the property owner or management to handle maintenance and repairs. This saves you the hassle and costs associated with home upkeep and ensures a stress-free living experience.

5.1.3 Mistakes To Avoid When Rushing To Buy

While the allure of owning property in Thailand can be tempting, it's crucial to approach it with caution and avoid rushing into a purchase. Some common mistakes expats make when hastily buying property include:

1. Insufficient research: Before making a purchase, thorough research is essential. Familiarize yourself with the local real estate market, legal requirements, and property ownership regulations. Seek professional advice and consider consulting a reputable lawyer or real estate agent.

2. Overextending financially: Buying property is a significant financial commitment. Be mindful of your budget and avoid overextending yourself. Consider your long-term financial goals and ensure that purchasing a property aligns with your overall financial plan.

3. Lack of familiarity with the area: Take the time to explore different neighborhoods and regions before committing to buying. What may seem appealing at first glance might not align with your lifestyle or preferences upon closer inspection. Renting in the area before buying can provide valuable insights.

In my own experience, renting for the first 10 years in places like Hua Hin and Phuket proved to be a wise decision. It allowed me the freedom to explore different areas, adapt to changing circumstances, and avoid potential pitfalls associated with rushed property purchases. Renting provided the flexibility I needed as I moved around for work, and I'm grateful I didn't rush into buying without a solid understanding of the local market.

Remember, buying property should be a carefully considered decision. Take your time, do your due diligence, and weigh the pros and cons of renting versus buying before making a commitment

5.2 Buying Property in Thailand: Opportunities and Pitfalls

W hen it comes to buying property in Thailand, there are several important considerations to keep in mind. As an expat who has never purchased a property, I have no direct experience but I can offer insights into the process, legal restrictions, and potential pitfalls to be aware of.

Foreigners in Thailand are restricted from owning land directly. However, there are legal ways to own property, such as condos, under your name or through a leasehold agreement. Condos provide a viable option for expats, as they offer ownership of the unit while the land remains under the ownership of a Thai entity. This is a popular choice for many foreigners looking to invest in property in Thailand.

However, it's crucial to be cautious and aware of potential scams or fraudulent practices when buying property. Unfortunately, there have been instances where unsuspecting foreigners have fallen victim to scams, losing their investment or facing legal complications. One particular area of concern is buying property off-plan.

Buying off-plan refers to purchasing a property before it is completed or even constructed. While this can present an opportunity to secure a property at a lower price or with favorable payment terms, it also carries inherent risks. Some buyers have faced challenges when developers fail to complete projects as promised, leading to financial losses and legal battles.

In recent years, there have been reported cases of buyers losing money due to stalled or abandoned off-plan projects. It is essential to thoroughly research and assess the credibility and track record of developers before committing to an off-plan purchase. Engaging professional advice, conducting background checks on the developer's previous projects, and reviewing the terms and conditions of the purchase agreement can help mitigate the risks associated with off-plan purchases.

Determining where to buy property in Thailand depends on your preferences and objectives. Popular destinations among expats include Bangkok, Phuket, Chiang Mai, and Pattaya. These areas offer diverse property options, ranging from luxurious beachfront villas to modern city condos. It's advisable to visit and explore different locations, assessing factors such as accessibility, amenities, and lifestyle suitability.

To ensure a smooth and legally sound property purchase, it is recommended to follow these steps:

1. Engage a reliable real estate agent or lawyer: Working with a reputable professional who understands the local market and legal requirements can greatly assist in the buying process.

2. Conduct thorough due diligence: Investigate the property's ownership status, title deeds, and any existing encumbrances. Verify that the seller has the legal right to sell the property.

3. Seek professional advice: Consult with a lawyer experienced in Thai property law to review contracts, negotiate terms, and ensure compliance with local regulations.

4. Understand financing options: Explore financing options available to foreigners in Thailand, as well as the associated costs and requirements.

5. Register the transaction: Once the purchase is complete, ensure that all necessary paperwork, including the transfer of ownership and registration, is properly executed and recorded.

Remember, buying property in Thailand is a significant investment, and careful consideration should be given to legal and financial aspects. By taking these precautions and seeking professional guidance, expats can navigate the property market with confidence and make informed decisions that align with their goals.

5.3 Exploring Rental Property Options: Villas, Condos, Townhouses, and More

When it comes to renting or buying a property in Thailand, you'll encounter a variety of options, each with its own set of pros and cons. Let's explore some popular choices and compare their features, prices, locations, and suitability based on your personality and preferences.

1. Villas:

- Pros: Villas offer spacious living areas, private gardens, and a sense of luxury and exclusivity. They are ideal for those seeking privacy, tranquility, and a connection with nature. Villas often come with amenities like swimming pools, outdoor spaces, and parking facilities.

- Cons: Villas are generally more expensive to rent or buy compared to condos or townhouses. They may require higher maintenance costs, and the availability of villas can be limited in certain areas, especially urban centers. They are more suitable for individuals or families who prioritize space, privacy, and a relaxed lifestyle.

2. Condos/Apartments:

- Pros: Condos provide convenience, amenities, and a sense of community. They are often located in prime areas with easy access to transportation, shopping centers, and entertainment. Condos typically offer facilities like gyms, swimming pools, and 24-hour security.

- Cons: Condos can have higher rental or purchase prices, especially in desirable locations. The space may be more limited compared to villas or townhouses. Noise levels and a more transient community can be potential drawbacks. Condos are suitable for those who prefer a modern lifestyle, access to amenities, and a bustling city environment.

3. Townhouses:

- Pros: Townhouses offer a balance between space, affordability, and community living. They often come with multiple floors, providing more living space compared to condos. Townhouses can be found in both urban and rural areas, offering a range of options.

- Cons: Townhouses may have limited outdoor space or garden areas compared to villas. Depending on the location, they may have shared walls, impacting privacy. Townhouses are suitable for individuals or families seeking a larger living area, a sense of community, and a more affordable option compared to villas.

4. Others (E.g., Shophouses, Traditional Houses):

- Pros: Thailand has a diverse range of unique properties, including shophouses, traditional houses, and converted spaces.

These properties offer a blend of culture, history, and character. They can be found in both urban and rural areas, providing a unique living experience.

- Cons: Availability and maintenance of these properties can vary. Some may require more extensive renovations or have limitations on modern amenities. These options are suitable for individuals who appreciate traditional architecture, cultural immersion, and a more unconventional living experience.

If having a garden is a priority, villas and some townhouses are excellent choices. Villas often come with ample outdoor space, allowing you to create your own oasis. Townhouses with private gardens or communal green spaces can also fulfill your desire for a garden setting. Condos may have shared or limited outdoor spaces, but they often compensate with communal facilities such as rooftop gardens or landscaped areas.

When considering rental prices, locations, and your personality, it's important to assess your budget, desired lifestyle, and proximity to amenities. Researching the rental market, consulting with real estate agents, and exploring different neighborhoods will help you find the best match for your needs.

Remember, everyone's preferences and requirements vary, so take your time to evaluate each option based on your desired living experience and financial considerations.

5.4 Buying Land in Thailand:
Legal Considerations, Superficies
Agreements, and Price Trends

I f you're considering buying land in Thailand, there are important legal considerations, options for ownership, and price trends to be aware of. Understanding these factors will help you navigate the process and make informed decisions.

5.4.1 Land Ownership And Personal Experience

In our personal experience, the land we built our farm on originally belonged to my wife before we met. We have also explored the possibility of purchasing surrounding areas for various purposes. It's worth noting that land ownership regulations differ for Thai nationals and foreigners.

5.4.2 Legal Considerations And Ownership Options

Thai Name or Company: Foreigners are generally restricted from owning land directly in Thailand. However, land can be owned by a Thai individual or a registered Thai company in which foreign ownership is limited to a maximum of 49%. Establishing a Thai company can be a complex process, and it's crucial to seek legal advice to ensure compliance with Thai laws and regulations.

Superficies Agreements: One way to protect yourself if buying land in a Thai name is through superficies agreements. This agreement grants the right to build and own structures on the land while separating ownership of the land itself. This provides more security and control over the property, but it's important to consult with a lawyer to draft a comprehensive agreement that safeguards your interests.

5.4.3 Price Differences And Trends

Price Variation: The price of land in Thailand varies significantly depending on location, accessibility, proximity to tourist areas, and development potential. Land in popular tourist destinations or urban centers tends to be more expensive compared to rural areas. Factors such as infrastructure, amenities, and scenic views also influence land prices.

Statistics and Examples: To provide a clearer picture, let's look at some statistics and example prices. In tourist areas like Phuket or Pattaya, beachfront land can range from 10 to 30 million baht per rai (1,600 square meters). In contrast, land in rural areas such as Buriram or Udon Thani can be as low as 100,000 to 300,000 baht per rai.

Price Trends: Over the years, land prices in Thailand have shown a general upward trend due to increased development and demand. However, it's important to note that price trends can vary by location and economic factors. Conducting thorough market research and seeking advice from local experts will provide valuable insights into specific areas of interest.

5.4.4 Conclusion And Recommendations

Buying land in Thailand requires careful consideration of legal requirements, ownership options, and market trends. Engaging a reputable lawyer with expertise in real estate transactions is essential to navigate the legal complexities and protect your interests. Additionally, staying updated on market trends and seeking advice from local professionals will help you make informed decisions.

Remember that every land purchase is unique, and it's crucial to evaluate individual circumstances, long-term goals, and financial feasibility before making a decision.

6. EMPLOYMENT AND BUSINESS OPPORTUNITIES

6.1: The Job Market in Thailand: Work Permits and Employment Opportunities

When considering working in Thailand as an expat, take some time to understand the job market dynamics and the requirement for work permits. In Thailand, you generally are not permitted to do a job that a Thai can do, by law. Finding employment in Thailand can be really challenging, and most expats typically find work in the education sector or the hospitality industry, many already have online work from International companies or their own entrepreneurial efforts, many of course are simply retired.

Teaching English as a foreign language is one of the most common avenues for expats seeking employment in Thailand. There is a high demand for English teachers, especially in private language schools, international schools, and universities. However, competition can be fierce, and qualifications such as a bachelor's degree and TEFL certification are often required. The pay is also often low ranging from just 15,000 THB to 50,000 THB for those without masters degrees or actual teaching qualifications. It is however a good way to break into the country, learn the language and culture before deciding to commit full-time.

Another popular sector for expat employment is the hospitality industry, which includes jobs in hotels, resorts, restaurants, and tourism-related businesses. Positions range from front-line staff to managerial roles. However, it's important to note that the hospitality industry can also be highly competitive, especially in popular tourist destinations.

I have had the opportunity to work as both a teacher and in the hospitality industry, specifically with Anantara Hotels. The job market in these fields was indeed highly competitive, with many qualified individuals vying for limited positions. It required a combination of relevant qualifications, experience, and networking to secure employment opportunities.

It's essential to understand that as an expat working in Thailand, a valid work permit is required. Work permits are granted by the Department of Employment and are usually sponsored by an employing company. The process can be complex, involving various documents, approvals, and fees. It's crucial to adhere to the regulations and ensure that your employment status is in compliance with Thai law. There is a huge grey area here with working online. In my experience many expats work online and keep it secretive with very little issue.

Networking and conducting thorough research are vital for increasing your chances of finding work in Thailand. Engage with local expat communities, attend job fairs, and join professional networks relevant to your field of interest. Additionally, explore online job portals and consult with reputable recruitment agencies that specialize in placing expats. It's important to be proactive, persistent, and open to opportunities that align with your skills and qualifications. In my experience knowing someone, or knowing someone that knows someone is often a good way to get a position.

Remember to stay informed about the latest regulations regarding work permits and ensure that your employment is legal and compliant. Seeking professional advice from immigration experts or consulting with the Department of Employment can provide you with accurate and up-to-date information regarding work permits and employment requirements.

Overall, while finding work in Thailand as an expat can be challenging, it's not impossible. With the right qualifications, a proactive approach, and a willingness to adapt, you can navigate the job market and explore rewarding career opportunities in the Land of Smiles.

6.2: Starting a Business in Thailand

Starting a business in Thailand involves specific procedures, costs, and potential challenges that need to be considered. As an entrepreneur who has registered two companies in

Thailand—a school and a bar—I have firsthand experience with the intricacies of starting and running businesses in the country. Let's delve into the specifics of registering a business, the associated expenses, potential pitfalls, and share some personal insights.

1. Business Registration Process and Company Structures:

The process of registering a business in Thailand involves several steps, including business name reservation, business registration, and tax and social security registration. Choosing the appropriate company structure is crucial, such as a Thai Limited Company or a Representative Office, depending on the nature of your business.

2. Costs Associated with Business Registration:

The costs of registering a business in Thailand can vary depending on factors such as the chosen company structure and required services. Government fees, legal and professional fees, and capital requirements need to be taken into account when budgeting for the registration process.

3. Pitfalls and Challenges:

Starting a business in Thailand comes with its fair share of challenges. Language and cultural barriers, regulatory compliance, and competition are among the hurdles entrepreneurs may face. It's crucial to understand and navigate these challenges to ensure a successful business venture.

4. Personal Experiences:

In my personal experience, I have found that the hospitality industry, including bars, can be particularly challenging in terms of generating consistent profits due to high competition and changing consumer preferences. Many Expats end up losing everything through starting a bar and not being able to keep it afloat. Thorough market research, a unique value proposition, and effective marketing strategies are essential to thrive in such industries.

5. Foreigners Doing Business In Thailand :

Statistics indicate that the number of registered foreign-owned companies in Thailand has been steadily increasing. However, it's important to carefully analyze the specific industry landscape, market demand, and competition before making any investment decisions.

Drawing from my own experiences, I emphasize the importance of conducting thorough market research, creating a solid business plan, seeking professional advice, and embracing innovative strategies to overcome challenges and succeed in the Thai business landscape.

When starting a business in Thailand, it's important to consider the costs involved. While the exact expenses can vary depending on the nature and scale of your business, here are some estimated costs to give you an idea:

1. Government fees: The registration fees for a company in Thailand can range from 5,000 to 10,000 baht, depending on the authorized capital of the company.

2. Legal and professional services: Hiring lawyers and accountants to assist with the registration process can range from 20,000 to 50,000 baht or more, depending on the complexity of your business and the scope of services required.

3. Capital requirements: The minimum capital requirement for a Thai limited company is 1 million baht, although this can be reduced for certain types of businesses. This is often just declared capitol, on paper only.

4. Office space: Renting an office space or commercial property

can vary greatly depending on the location and size. In Bangkok, office rents can range from 500 to 1,500 baht per square meter per month, while in other cities or provinces, the prices can be lower.

5. Utilities and operational costs: Monthly expenses for utilities such as electricity, water, and internet can range from 5,000 to 10,000 baht, depending on the size and nature of your business.

It's important to note that these estimates are approximate and can vary based on various factors. Engaging the services of experienced lawyers and accountants will ensure accurate estimates tailored to your specific business requirements.

To save money when starting a business in Thailand, it can be beneficial to consider using lawyers or accountants outside of Bangkok. While Bangkok-based professionals may have higher fees due to the city's higher cost of living and market demand, seeking services from professionals in other cities or provinces can potentially offer cost savings.

Engaging lawyers or accountants in areas with lower overhead costs may result in more competitive rates for their services. Additionally, they can still provide the necessary expertise and knowledge of Thai business laws and regulations, ensuring a smooth and compliant registration process for your business.

By widening your search and considering professionals from various locations, you can explore cost-effective options without compromising the quality of services. It's advisable to research and compare fees, qualifications, and track records of different professionals to make an informed decision that best fits your budget and requirements.

6.3: Working Online and Remote Work Options in Thailand

Working online has become increasingly popular, offering individuals the flexibility to work remotely and explore different job opportunities. However, it's important to understand the legal landscape surrounding online work in Thailand, as it can be a bit of a grey area and the Thai government have not explicitly addressed what is and is not allowed.

In terms of teaching, many expats have found online teaching positions to be a viable option. English language instruction, in particular, is in demand, and platforms like VIPKid, iTutorGroup, and Teach Away provide opportunities to teach English to students around the world. I have known many expats that live off teaching online and do not have a work permit, I have met others that subsidize their real teaching with online teaching. The general view on this as of writing is that the Thai government are not overly concerned with online teachers but you probably shouldn't advertise the fact you do it.

Another avenue for remote work is creating content on platforms like YouTube or other social media platforms. Sharing your expertise, skills, or experiences through video content can be a rewarding way to generate income. This has become our life here in Buriram of course. This is again a grey area with little clarity on whether a work permit is required or now If you have another business you can add YouTube to your work permit to be sure to be legal, as of writing the Thai government are not demanding work permits but this could well change, and fast!

When it comes to remote work options beyond teaching or content creation, freelancing and digital nomad opportunities exist in various fields such as graphic design, programming, writing, and marketing. Platforms like Upwork, Freelancer, and Fiverr provide avenues to connect with clients worldwide and offer your services remotely.

To stay on the right side of the law while working online in Thailand, it's advisable to consult with a lawyer or accountant who can provide guidance on legal obligations, tax implications, and visa requirements. As the legal landscape surrounding online work is constantly evolving, seeking professional advice can help ensure compliance and mitigate any potential risks, but you may find there are few answers and, without a company address, correct visa and work permit, anything that generates income in the kingdom is classed as working and therefore technically illegal.

6.4: Freelancing and Consulting in Thailand

F or individuals considering a move to Thailand, freelancing and consulting can be lucrative and fulfilling options for work. Thailand offers a vibrant and dynamic market that welcomes independent professionals with specialized skills and expertise. Engaging in freelance work or providing consulting services can provide flexibility, autonomy, and the opportunity to work with diverse clients both locally and internationally.

Freelancing in Thailand allows you to leverage your talents and offer services in various fields, such as content writing, graphic design, web development, digital marketing, and more. The demand for freelancers is high, particularly in industries related to technology, creative arts, and digital media. Through online platforms, networking, and building a strong portfolio, you can establish your presence and attract clients who value your skills.

Consulting is another avenue worth exploring. Sharing your knowledge and experiences can be valuable for individuals and businesses seeking expert guidance. Whether it's advising on relocating to Thailand, starting a business, or building an online presence through platforms like YouTube, consulting offers the opportunity to offer tailored advice and solutions to clients who may require specialized expertise.

One of the advantages of freelancing and consulting in Thailand is the lower cost of living compared to Western countries. This allows you to maintain a comfortable lifestyle while potentially earning competitive rates for your services. Additionally, Thailand's strategic location and growing economy create opportunities to work with local businesses as well as international clients.

To succeed as a freelancer or consultant in Thailand, it is crucial to build a strong professional network, showcase your skills and expertise through online platforms and marketing channels, and continually develop your knowledge in your respective field. Attending industry events, joining relevant communities, and staying updated with market trends can help you stay competitive and attract new clients.

When pursuing freelancing or consulting in Thailand, it's essential to consider legal requirements, such as acquiring the necessary visas and work permits. Consulting a local lawyer or accountant who specializes in assisting freelancers and consultants can provide guidance on the legal aspects and ensure compliance with Thai regulations.

Thailand's thriving economy, diverse business landscape, and supportive digital community make it an attractive destination for freelancers and consultants. By offering your expertise, embracing the local culture, and seizing opportunities to network, you can enjoy the rewards of a flexible and fulfilling professional journey while embracing the unique experiences Thailand has to offer.

7. GETTING AROUND IN THAILAND

7.1: Getting Around in Thailand

T ransportation plays a vital role in navigating the diverse landscapes of Thailand. Whether you're exploring the bustling city streets or cruising through the scenic countryside, having reliable transportation can greatly enhance your experience. In this section, we'll discuss various modes of transportation and share some insights based on our recent experience.

Firstly, we're excited to share that we recently added a new car to our farm. Having a car in a rural area like ours provides convenience and flexibility, allowing us to easily access nearby towns, markets, and other amenities. It also gives us the freedom to explore the beautiful countryside at our own pace. Plus, it has been a wonderful opportunity for my wife, Damo, to learn how to drive and gain independence.

In Thailand, there are several options for transportation beyond owning a car. Public transportation networks are well-established, particularly in major cities like Bangkok, where you can rely on a combination of buses, trains, and taxis to get around.

Additionally, motorcycle taxis and tuk-tuks are popular choices for shorter distances or navigating through congested traffic.

For those who prefer a more eco-friendly approach, bicycles are a fantastic way to explore smaller towns and scenic areas. They offer a leisurely and immersive experience, allowing you to soak in the sights, sounds, and culture of Thailand at a slower pace.

Owning a car provides convenience and privacy, especially in rural areas with limited public transportation options. However, it comes with the responsibility of maintenance, parking, tax, insurance and adherence to traffic regulations.

On the other hand, public transportation can be cost-effective and efficient, particularly in urban areas where traffic congestion is common. It's a great way to immerse yourself in the local culture, interact with fellow commuters, and navigate through bustling city streets. However, it may require some familiarity with the routes and schedules

7.2: Road Safety in Thailand

While Thailand offers a diverse and exciting transportation landscape, it's important to be aware of road safety considerations. Like any country, Thailand has its own unique road conditions and challenges. In this section, we'll touch upon some road safety statistics and offer tips to help you stay safe on the roads.

It's important to note that road accidents are a significant concern in Thailand. According to statistics, the country has one of the highest road traffic fatality rates in the world. Factors such as reckless driving, inadequate enforcement of traffic laws, and a lack of road safety awareness contribute to this unfortunate situation.

To ensure your safety while traveling on Thai roads, here are some important tips to keep in mind:

1. Observe Traffic Laws: Familiarize yourself with local traffic regulations and adhere to them at all times. This includes following speed limits, wearing seat belts, having valid licenses and using helmets when riding motorcycles.

2. Defensive Driving: Practice defensive driving techniques to anticipate and respond to potential hazards on the road. Maintain a safe distance from other vehicles, use your mirrors frequently, and stay alert to your surroundings.

3. Be Mindful of Motorcycles: Motorcycles are a common mode of transportation in Thailand. Exercise caution and be attentive to motorcyclists on the road. Give them ample space and avoid sudden maneuvers that may endanger their safety.

4. Stay Sober: Never drink and drive. Operating a vehicle under the influence of alcohol or drugs is not only illegal but also poses a serious risk to yourself and others on the road.

5. Stay Updated on Road Conditions: Keep informed about road conditions, particularly during adverse weather or during holidays when traffic volume may be high. Plan your journeys accordingly and allow for extra time if needed.

Remember, road safety is a shared responsibility. By adopting safe driving practices, being aware of potential risks, and respecting local traffic laws, you can contribute to a safer transportation environment for yourself and others.

While road safety is an important consideration, it should not discourage you from exploring the beauty and wonders of Thailand. With proper awareness and caution, you can enjoy your travels and make lasting memories while prioritizing your well-being on the road.

7.3: Driving in Thailand - Licenses and Road Rules

Driving in Thailand can be an exciting way to explore the country's diverse landscapes and vibrant cities. However, it's important to familiarize yourself with the necessary licenses and road rules to ensure a safe and enjoyable driving experience. In this section, we will discuss driving licenses, traffic regulations, and road safety in Thailand.

1. Driving Licenses:

To legally drive in Thailand, you must have a valid driver's license issued by the Department of Land Transport (DLT). The requirements for obtaining a Thai driver's license may vary depending on your nationality and current driving license. Here are the key points to consider:

- International Driving Permit (IDP): If you hold a valid IDP or an equivalent driving license from your home country, you can use it for driving in Thailand for a limited period. However, it is recommended to obtain a Thai driver's license for longer stays.

- Converting Foreign License: Some countries have agreements with Thailand, allowing their citizens to convert their foreign driver's licenses to a Thai driver's license. The conversion process typically involves submitting required documents, undergoing a vision test, and paying the necessary fees.

- Thai Driver's License: If you do not have a valid international or converted license, you will need to obtain a Thai driver's license by passing the written and practical driving tests conducted by the DLT.

2. Traffic Regulations:

Understanding and adhering to the traffic regulations in Thailand is crucial for safe driving. Here are some important road rules to keep in mind:

- Drive on the left: Similar to many other countries, Thailand follows left-hand driving. The steering wheel is on the right side of the vehicle, and traffic moves on the left side of the road.

- Speed Limits: The speed limits in Thailand vary depending on the type of road and location. In urban areas, the speed limit is usually 60 km/h (37 mph), while on highways, it can range from 90 km/h (56 mph) to 120 km/h (75 mph).

- Seat Belts and Helmets: Both drivers and passengers are required to wear seat belts in vehicles equipped with them. Motorcyclists and their passengers must wear helmets at all times.

- Traffic Signs and Signals: Familiarize yourself with the various traffic signs, signals, and road markings used in Thailand. These provide important information, warnings, and guidance while driving.

7.4: Motorbikes, Accidents, and Legal Consequences

Motorbikes are a popular means of transportation in Thailand, offering convenience and flexibility. However, it's important to be aware of the associated risks, road safety measures, and legal consequences. In this section, we will discuss motorbike rentals, accidents, and potential legal issues related to riding in Thailand.

1. Motorbike Rentals:

Renting a motorbike in Thailand is a common choice for many travelers and expatriates. Here are some key points to consider:

- Rental Requirements: Rental agencies typically require a valid driver's license and a passport. Some may also ask for a deposit or keep your passport until the bike is returned.

- Safety Gear: It is essential to wear appropriate safety gear, including a helmet, when riding a motorbike. Rental agencies usually provide helmets, but it's advisable to bring your own for better comfort and hygiene.

- Bike Inspection: Before renting a motorbike, carefully inspect its condition, including the brakes, lights, tires, and overall functionality. Report any pre-existing damages to the rental agency to avoid disputes later.

2. Accidents and Injuries:

Motorbike accidents are unfortunately common in Thailand, and injuries can range from minor to severe. To minimize the risk of accidents and injuries, consider the following:

- Defensive Riding: Practice defensive riding techniques, maintain a safe distance from other vehicles, and anticipate potential hazards on the road.

- Observe Traffic Laws: Adhere to traffic laws and regulations, including speed limits, traffic signals, and lane discipline.

- Be Alert and Visible: Stay alert and maintain visibility by using headlights, signal lights, and reflective gear, especially during low-light conditions.

- Avoid Intoxicated Riding: Never operate a motorbike while under the influence of alcohol or drugs. Impaired riding greatly increases the risk of accidents.

3. Legal Consequences:

In recent years, Thai authorities have increased enforcement of traffic laws, especially in popular tourist areas. Here are some important legal considerations:

- Helmet Requirement: It is mandatory to wear a helmet while riding a motorbike in Thailand. Failing to do so can result in fines imposed by the police.

- License and Documentation: Always carry a valid driver's license, either an international driving permit or a Thai driver's license. Failure to produce a license when asked by authorities can lead to fines.

- Deportation Risk: In certain tourist destinations, such as Phuket, authorities have been cracking down on unlicensed riders and those who violate traffic laws. Offenders may face fines, legal proceedings, or even deportation in some cases.

- Insurance Coverage: Ensure you have appropriate insurance coverage that includes motorbike accidents. Check with your insurance provider to confirm coverage and any specific requirements.

Familiarize yourself with the local traffic rules, wear safety gear, and exercise caution on the roads to minimize the risk of accidents and legal consequences.

8. EXPERIENCING THAI CUISINE AND LOCAL DELIGHTS

8.1: Introduction to Thai Cuisine

As you embark on your journey to experience the vibrant culture of Thailand, one aspect that you cannot afford to miss is the delightful Thai cuisine. Known for its bold flavors, fresh ingredients, and unique combinations, Thai cuisine offers a culinary adventure that will tantalize your taste buds and leave you craving for more. In this section, I will provide an introduction to Thai cuisine, giving you a glimpse into the diverse and flavorful world of local delights.

1. Flavors and Ingredients:

Thai cuisine is characterized by a harmonious balance of flavors, combining sweet, sour, salty, spicy, and sometimes bitter elements in each dish. The use of fresh herbs, aromatic spices, and a variety of vegetables and proteins contribute to the richness and complexity of Thai flavors. From tangy lime and lemongrass to fiery chili peppers and fragrant basil, the ingredients used in Thai cooking create a symphony of tastes.

2. Signature Dishes:

Thai cuisine boasts a range of signature dishes that have gained international acclaim. Here are some must-try dishes:

- Pad Thai: A stir-fried noodle dish with a perfect blend of sweet, savory, and tangy flavors, featuring rice noodles, shrimp or chicken, eggs, tofu, bean sprouts, and crushed peanuts.

- Tom Yum Goong: A hot and sour soup that tantalizes the taste buds with its combination of lemongrass, galangal, lime leaves, chili, and succulent shrimp.

- Green Curry (Kaeng Khiao Wan): A creamy and aromatic curry made with green chili paste, coconut milk, vegetables, and your choice of meat or seafood.

- Massaman Curry: A mild and fragrant curry influenced by Indian spices, typically prepared with tender chunks of meat, potatoes, and roasted peanuts.

- Som Tam: A refreshing and spicy papaya salad featuring shredded green papaya, tomatoes, green beans, peanuts, and a zesty dressing.

3. Street Food Culture:

Thailand is renowned for its vibrant street food culture, where you can find an array of delectable treats and local delights. From sizzling stir-fries and aromatic soups to grilled skewers and tropical fruit shakes, the streets of Thailand offer a sensory feast for food enthusiasts. Exploring the bustling street markets and night bazaars will expose you to a wide variety of mouthwatering dishes that reflect the country's culinary heritage.

4. Dietary Considerations:

Thai cuisine offers options for various dietary preferences and restrictions. Whether you prefer vegetarian or vegan dishes, or if you have gluten or seafood allergies, you can find suitable choices in Thai cuisine. Many restaurants and food stalls are accommodating and willing to customize dishes to meet specific dietary needs. However, it's always helpful to communicate your requirements clearly to ensure a satisfying dining experience.

Thai cuisine is not just about the flavors; it's also about the communal dining experience and the warmth of Thai hospitality. So, as you venture into the world of Thai cuisine, embrace the diverse flavors, explore the local markets, and engage with the friendly locals who will be delighted to introduce you to their culinary traditions. Get ready to embark on a gastronomic journey filled with unforgettable flavors and culinary delights in the land of smiles.

8.2: Exploring Local Markets and Street Food

One of the best ways to immerse yourself in Thai culture and experience the true essence of local life is by exploring the bustling markets and savoring the mouthwatering street food. Thailand is renowned for its vibrant market scenes, where you can find an abundance of fresh produce, aromatic spices, and an array of delectable street food options. In this section, we will delve into the world of Thai markets and street food, offering you a glimpse into the lively and flavorful experiences that await you.

1. Local Markets:

Thai markets are vibrant hubs of activity, offering a diverse range of goods and culinary treasures. From sprawling night markets to morning fresh markets, each has its own unique charm. Stroll through the aisles and soak in the vibrant atmosphere as locals haggle for the best deals and vendors proudly display their colorful array of fruits, vegetables, herbs, and spices. Take your time to explore the market stalls and discover exotic ingredients that you may have never encountered before.

2. Street Food Delights:

Thailand's street food scene is legendary, with countless vendors serving up tantalizing dishes that showcase the country's culinary prowess. From fragrant noodle soups and sizzling stir-fries to grilled satay skewers and crispy spring rolls, the options are endless. The sizzle of woks, the aroma of herbs and spices, and the sight of skillful cooks whipping up dishes right before your eyes create an exciting and dynamic dining experience.

3. Must-Try Street Food:

When it comes to street food in Thailand, there are some iconic dishes that you simply must try:

- Mango Sticky Rice (Khao Niew Mamuang): A classic Thai dessert featuring ripe mango slices served with sweet glutinous rice drizzled with coconut cream.

- Grilled Chicken (Gai Yang): Tender and flavorful grilled chicken marinated in a blend of aromatic herbs and spices, served with sticky rice and spicy dipping sauces.

- Fried Pad Thai Noodles: A beloved Thai street food staple, featuring stir-fried rice noodles with shrimp, tofu, eggs, bean sprouts, and crushed peanuts.

- Grilled Pork Skewers (Moo Ping): Succulent and marinated pork skewers grilled to perfection and served with a tangy dipping sauce.

- Thai Iced Tea (Cha Yen): A refreshing and sweet beverage made from black tea, condensed milk, and served over ice.

4. Exploring with Caution:

While Thai street food offers a fantastic culinary adventure, it's important to exercise caution to ensure a safe and enjoyable experience. Here are a few tips to keep in mind:

- Choose stalls with a high turnover of customers, as it indicates fresh and popular food.
- Ensure that food is cooked thoroughly and served hot to minimize the risk of foodborne illnesses.
- Opt for bottled water or freshly squeezed fruit juices to stay hydrated.
- If you have any dietary restrictions or allergies, communicate your needs clearly to the vendors.
- Use your judgment and observe the cleanliness and hygiene practices of the food stalls.

Exploring local markets and savoring street food is not just about the food itself; it's a cultural experience that allows you to connect with the heart and soul of Thailand. Engage with the friendly vendors, try new flavors, and embrace the vibrant street food culture. Whether you're enjoying a quick snack on the go or indulging in a full meal, the culinary delights of Thai markets and street food are sure to leave a lasting impression on your taste buds and create cherished memories of your time in Thailand.

8.3: Exploring Unique Regional Specialties

T hailand's culinary landscape is incredibly diverse, with each region boasting its own distinct flavors and specialties. In this section, we will delve into the unique regional cuisines of Thailand, focusing particularly on the delightful dishes found in Buriram and the northeastern region, known as Isan.

1. Isan Cuisine:

Isan cuisine, originating from the northeastern part of Thailand, offers a bold and vibrant culinary experience. It is characterized by its spicy, tangy, and herbaceous flavors, showcasing the use of local ingredients and traditional cooking techniques. One of the most beloved Isan dishes is "Som Tam," a refreshing papaya salad that combines the perfect balance of sour, spicy, and sweet flavors. Made with shredded green papaya, chili, garlic, lime juice, fish sauce, and palm sugar, it's a favorite among locals and visitors alike. Isan cuisine also features grilled meats, spicy soups, and flavorful dips that pair perfectly with sticky rice.

2. Buriram Delights:

As you explore the local cuisine in Buriram, you'll discover a range of delightful dishes that reflect the region's agricultural heritage and cultural influences. Some popular Buriram specialties include:

- Koi Pla: A traditional fish salad made with raw, finely chopped fish mixed with fresh herbs, lime juice, chili, and fish sauce. It offers a burst of zesty flavors and is often enjoyed with sticky rice.

- Khao Yam: A colorful rice salad that combines fragrant herbs, vegetables, shredded coconut, and a tangy dressing. It's a light and refreshing dish, perfect for a warm day.

- Moo Yang: Grilled pork marinated in a flavorful blend of spices and served with a dipping sauce. The smoky and juicy pork pairs well with sticky rice and a side of fresh vegetables.

- Gaeng Ranjuan: A spicy and aromatic curry with tender meat, fragrant herbs, and rich spices. It's a comforting dish that showcases the unique flavors of the region.

3. Exploring Local Eateries:

To truly experience the regional specialties, venture into local eateries and street food stalls in Buriram. These establishments offer an authentic taste of the local flavors, often prepared by skilled cooks who have honed their recipes over generations. Engage with the locals, seek their recommendations, and be open to trying new dishes that may be unique to the region.

4. Embracing the Culinary Adventure:

As you indulge in the regional specialties of Buriram and Isan, let your taste buds guide you on a culinary adventure. Explore the flavors, textures, and aromas that make each dish unique. From the fiery spiciness of chili to the aromatic blend of herbs and spices, every bite tells a story of the region's culinary heritage.

Don't miss the opportunity to try different variations of Som Tam, as each vendor may have their own twist on this beloved salad. Embrace the bold flavors, embrace the authenticity, and savor the culinary journey through the local specialties of Buriram and Isan.

Remember, exploring regional specialties allows you to uncover the rich tapestry of flavors that Thailand has to offer. So, don't be afraid to venture beyond the familiar and discover the hidden gems of Buriram's culinary scene.

8.4: Dining Etiquette and Cultural Considerations

W hen experiencing Thai cuisine and local delights in Thailand, it's important to be mindful of dining etiquette and cultural considerations. Thai culture places great emphasis on politeness, respect, and communal dining. Here are some tips to enhance your dining experiences and show appreciation for the local customs:

1. Greetings and Respect:

In Thai culture, showing respect is essential. When entering a restaurant or someone's home, it's customary to greet the host or staff with a polite "wai" (placing your palms together in a prayer-like gesture) and a warm smile. This gesture is a sign of respect and acknowledgment.

2. Sharing and Communal Dining:

Thai meals are often enjoyed in a communal style, where several dishes are shared among everyone at the table. It's common to order a variety of dishes and share them with others. Remember to wait for the host or eldest person to initiate the meal or invite you to start eating before you begin.

3. Chopsticks and Utensils:

While chopsticks are commonly used in many Asian countries, Thai cuisine is primarily enjoyed with a fork and spoon. The fork is held in the left hand to push food onto the spoon, which is held in the right hand for eating. Chopsticks may be provided for certain dishes, especially noodle soups, but using utensils is the norm.

4. Tasting and Appreciating Flavors:

Thai cuisine is renowned for its intricate blend of flavors, balancing spicy, sweet, sour, and savory tastes. Take your time to savor each dish, appreciating the different flavors and textures. It's common to mix different dishes together, combining flavors according to your personal preference.

5. Spiciness and Heat:

Thai cuisine is known for its spiciness, and chili peppers are frequently used in many dishes. If you're not accustomed to spicy food, it's perfectly acceptable to request milder versions of certain dishes. Communicate your spice tolerance to the waitstaff, and they will gladly accommodate your preference.

6. Eating Mindfully:

Thai culture emphasizes the importance of mindfulness in all aspects of life, including eating. Take the time to eat slowly and savor each bite. Engage in conversation with your dining companions and enjoy the social aspect of the meal.

7. Gratitude and Compliments:

At the end of the meal, it's customary to express gratitude to the host or restaurant staff. A simple "khop khun" (thank you) is a thoughtful gesture to show your appreciation for the delicious meal and hospitality.

By observing these cultural considerations, you can enhance your dining experiences and show respect for Thai customs. Embrace the communal nature of Thai cuisine, explore new flavors, and engage in the rich culinary traditions of the country. Enjoy the vibrant and diverse world of Thai cuisine, one delightful bite at a time.

9. EXPLORING THAILAND'S NATURAL BEAUTY

9.1: Exploring Hidden Gems and Must-Visit Destinations

T hailand is a treasure trove of hidden gems and must-visit destinations, offering a diverse range of experiences for travelers. Whether you're seeking natural wonders, cultural sites, or off-the-beaten-path adventures, Thailand has something to offer. Here are a few remarkable places, some of which we have documented on our YouTube channel, that you should consider adding to your itinerary:

1. Koh Sok:

One of my personal favorite spots is Koh Sok, a pristine national park located in southern Thailand. Known for its breathtaking limestone cliffs, crystal-clear lakes, and lush rainforests, Koh Sok offers a unique opportunity to immerse yourself in nature. Explore the park's stunning Cheow Lan Lake, go hiking through the dense jungle, or embark on a memorable overnight stay in a floating bungalow. Koh Sok is a true gem that showcases the beauty of Thailand's natural landscapes.

2. Koh Chang Noi:

If you're looking for a secluded and lesser-known island experience, consider visiting Koh Chang Noi. Located in the Andaman Sea, this tiny island is a tranquil haven away from the crowds. With its pristine beaches, crystal-clear waters, and untouched natural beauty, Koh Chang Noi is perfect for those seeking a peaceful retreat. Relax on the sandy shores, snorkel in the vibrant coral reefs, and immerse yourself in the laid-back atmosphere of this hidden paradise. I often stay with Mr Oh at Hornbill bungalows!

These are just a couple of examples of the many incredible destinations that Thailand has to offer. Whether you're a nature lover, a culture enthusiast, or an adventurer at heart, Thailand's diverse landscapes and attractions will leave you in awe. Don't hesitate to explore beyond the well-trodden tourist paths and discover the hidden gems that await you.

Remember to check out our YouTube channel, where we have documented some of these remarkable places, providing you with visual insights and practical tips for your future travels. From stunning national parks to lesser-known islands, our channel aims to inspire and guide you in your exploration of Thailand's hidden treasures.

9.2: Pristine Beaches and Coastal Getaways: Exploring Thailand's Serene Locations

T hailand's coastline is adorned with a plethora of pristine beaches and coastal retreats, each offering its own unique charm and allure. If you seek tranquil and picturesque destinations, here are some exceptional locations to consider:

1. Koh Lanta:

Situated in the Andaman Sea, Koh Lanta beckons with its unspoiled beaches, turquoise waters, and lush greenery. This peaceful island is renowned for its laid-back atmosphere and is an ideal spot for relaxation and rejuvenation. Enjoy long walks on its sandy shores, witness stunning sunsets, and indulge in the island's tantalizing seafood cuisine.

2. Koh Chang:

Nestled in the Gulf of Thailand, Koh Chang is one of the country's largest islands and boasts stunning beaches, pristine rainforests, and cascading waterfalls. Adventure enthusiasts can explore the island's hiking trails, kayak through mangrove forests, or dive into vibrant coral reefs. For a serene and untouched coastal experience, head to the eastern side of the island where tranquility reigns.

3. Railay Beach:

Accessible only by boat, Railay Beach is a hidden gem located near Krabi. Encircled by towering limestone cliffs, this beach paradise offers a unique blend of natural beauty and adventure. Embark on rock climbing adventures, explore hidden caves, or simply bask in the sun on its powder-soft sands. Railay Beach is renowned for its stunning vistas and serene ambiance.

4. Koh Phi Phi:

Known for its captivating beauty and crystal-clear waters, Koh Phi Phi has become an iconic destination in Thailand. This group of islands offers breathtaking viewpoints, vibrant marine life for snorkeling or diving, and a lively nightlife scene. Don't miss the famous Maya Bay, featured in the movie "The Beach," which showcases the stunning allure of this tropical paradise.

5. Khanom:

For a quieter coastal escape, head to Khanom, a serene and less touristy destination in southern Thailand. It is known for its long stretches of pristine beaches, where you can enjoy peaceful walks and observe rare pink dolphins playing in the sea. Khanom offers a tranquil retreat away from the crowds and a chance to immerse yourself in nature's beauty.

These are just a few examples of the many pristine beaches and coastal getaways Thailand has to offer. Each destination boasts its own unique offerings, whether it's the majestic cliffs of Railay Beach, the vibrant marine life of Koh Phi Phi, or the untouched serenity of Khanom. Explore these enchanting locations, embrace their natural wonders, and create unforgettable memories in Thailand's coastal paradises.

9.3: Trekking and Nature Trails

W hen it comes to exploring the natural wonders of Thailand, trekking and nature trails offer a thrilling way to connect with the country's diverse landscapes and ecosystems. Solo travelers seeking adventure and solitude will find an array of stunning destinations to satisfy their wanderlust. Here are some top spots for trekking and nature enthusiasts, each with its own unique attributes:

1. Doi Inthanon, Chiang Mai: Known as the "Roof of Thailand," Doi Inthanon is the highest peak in the country. Trekking through its misty trails allows you to experience breathtaking panoramas of lush greenery, vibrant flora, and cascading waterfalls. Nature lovers will also be delighted by the opportunity to spot rare bird species, including the stunning Green-tailed Sunbird and the endemic White-browed Shortwing.

2. Khao Sok National Park, Surat Thani: Nestled in the heart of southern Thailand, Khao Sok National Park is a true gem for nature enthusiasts. Its ancient rainforests, limestone formations, and the magnificent Cheow Lan Lake offer a perfect backdrop for trekking and exploration. Guided treks through the park's verdant trails unveil hidden waterfalls, vibrant wildlife, and the chance to witness the iconic Rafflesia, the world's largest flower.

3. Erawan National Park, Kanchanaburi: Situated in western Thailand, Erawan National Park is famous for its enchanting emerald green pools and the multi-tiered Erawan Waterfall. Trekking through the park allows you to marvel at the cascading falls and relax in the refreshing waters. Keep an eye out for playful monkeys swinging from the trees and colorful bird species fluttering amidst the foliage.

4. Phu Chi Fa, Chiang Rai: Located on the border with Laos, Phu Chi

Fa offers a unique trekking experience with its stunning sunrise vistas. Rising early and embarking on a hike to the viewpoint rewards you with breathtaking views of the sea of mist blanketing the surrounding valleys. As the sun emerges on the horizon, the landscape is bathed in hues of orange and gold, creating a truly magical sight.

5. Doi Suthep-Pui National Park, Chiang Mai: This sprawling national park is a haven for hikers and nature lovers. The highlight is the iconic Doi Suthep Temple, perched atop a mountain with sweeping views of Chiang Mai city below. Trekking through the park's lush trails allows you to witness an array of flora and fauna, including the vibrant rhododendron flowers and elusive wildlife like gibbons and macaques.

6. Khao Yai National Park, Nakhon Ratchasima: As Thailand's oldest and most renowned national park, Khao Yai offers a diverse range of trekking opportunities. From dense jungles to grassy plains and towering waterfalls, the park's trails lead you through a rich tapestry of landscapes. Wildlife enthusiasts will be thrilled by the chance to spot elephants, deer, hornbills, and even the elusive Asian black bear.

7. Sai Yok National Park, Kanchanaburi: Located in the picturesque province of Kanchanaburi, Sai Yok National Park boasts stunning waterfalls, limestone caves, and tranquil river rafting opportunities. Trekking along its scenic trails allows you to marvel at the cascading Sai Yok Noi Waterfall, explore the awe-inspiring Lawa Cave, and witness the impressive Sai Yok Yai Waterfall.

These are just a few examples of the remarkable trekking and nature destinations in Thailand.

9.4: Waterfalls, Caves, and Adventure Sports

Thailand's natural beauty extends beyond its pristine beaches and lush forests. The country is also home to breathtaking waterfalls, captivating caves, and thrilling adventure sports. Whether you seek the rush of adrenaline or a serene encounter with nature, there are plenty of options to explore. Here are some top recommendations for waterfalls, caves, and adventure sports enthusiasts:

1. Erawan Waterfall, Kanchanaburi: Situated in Erawan National Park, this seven-tiered waterfall is renowned for its crystal-clear turquoise pools. Hiking through the park's trails allows you to discover each tier, with the opportunity to swim and relax in the refreshing waters. The cascading falls and lush surroundings create a picturesque setting for nature lovers.

2. Tham Lod Cave, Mae Hong Son: Located in the northwestern province of Mae Hong Son, Tham Lod Cave offers a unique adventure. As you navigate its limestone chambers with a local guide, marvel at the stalactite formations, ancient rock paintings, and the awe-inspiring natural beauty. You can even take a bamboo raft ride along the underground river that flows through the cave.

3. Erawan Cave, Nakhon Nayok: This hidden gem is nestled within the Khao Chamao-Khao Wong National Park. Accessible only by boat, Erawan Cave enchants visitors with its shimmering stalactites and stalagmites, forming intricate patterns that resemble a mythical dragon. Exploring the cavernous chambers is an unforgettable experience.

4. Adventure Sports in Pai: The charming town of Pai, nestled in the mountains of northern Thailand, is a hub for adventure sports. You can indulge in adrenaline-pumping activities such as white-water rafting along the Pai River, zip-lining through the treetops, or off-road biking along scenic trails. The rugged terrain and stunning landscapes add to the thrill of these outdoor adventures.

5. Chiang Mai Flight of the Gibbon: For an exhilarating treetop adventure, head to Chiang Mai's Flight of the Gibbon. This zipline course takes you soaring through the lush jungle canopy, offering breathtaking views and an adrenaline rush. It's a fantastic way to experience the natural beauty of Thailand from a unique

perspective.

6. Krabi Rock Climbing: With its towering limestone cliffs, Krabi is a mecca for rock climbing enthusiasts. Whether you're a beginner or an experienced climber, there are routes suitable for all levels. Ascend the impressive cliffs, conquer challenging routes, and soak in the awe-inspiring vistas of the Andaman Sea and lush surroundings.

7. Kanchanaburi Jungle Rafts: Immerse yourself in a unique floating accommodation experience at Kanchanaburi Jungle Rafts. These traditional floating bamboo houses situated on the River Kwai offer a peaceful retreat surrounded by nature. You can enjoy river swimming, bamboo rafting, and even witness the enchanting sight of fireflies illuminating the night sky.

These are just a few examples of the thrilling waterfalls, captivating caves, and adventurous sports activities that await you in Thailand. From exploring hidden caves to cascading down waterfalls or embarking on adrenaline-fueled adventures, the country offers a multitude of unforgettable experiences for every adventure seeker.

10. EMBRACING THE THAI LIFESTYLE

10.1: Thai Language and Basic Phrases

One of the keys to truly embracing the Thai lifestyle is learning the Thai language. Communication becomes easier, and it allows you to connect more deeply with the local culture. Here are some insights into learning Thai and essential phrases to get you started:

1. Learning Thai as a Teacher: When I first came to live in Thailand, I worked as a teacher, which provided an excellent opportunity to learn the Thai language. Being in a classroom setting and interacting with students and colleagues helped me practice and improve my language skills. If you have the chance to work as a teacher or in a similar environment, it can be a rewarding way to learn Thai.

2. Immersion: Immersing yourself in the Thai language is one of the most effective ways to learn. Surrounding yourself with the language and using it in everyday situations helps you pick up vocabulary and improve your pronunciation. Engaging in conversations with locals, watching Thai TV shows or movies,

and listening to Thai music are all immersive experiences that can enhance your language learning journey.

3. Language Exchange: Language exchange programs provide an opportunity to practice Thai with native speakers while helping them learn your language. You can find language exchange partners through online platforms, language schools, or local meetups. This allows you to practice speaking and gain cultural insights from a native speaker.

4. Thai Language Schools: Joining a Thai language school is another option to learn Thai. These schools offer structured courses taught by experienced instructors. They provide a comprehensive curriculum that covers grammar, vocabulary, reading, writing, and speaking skills. Attending classes in a supportive environment can accelerate your learning and provide a solid foundation in the language.

5. Basic Words and Phrases: Here are some essential Thai words and phrases to get you started:

- Hello: Sawasdee (sa-wat-dee)
- Thank you: Khob khun (kob-koon)
- Yes: Chai (chai)
- No: Mai chai (mai-chai)
- How are you?: Sabai dee mai? (sa-bai-dee mai)
- Excuse me: Kor thot (kor-tot)
- I don't understand: Mai khao jai (mai kao jai)
- Please: Karuna (ka-roon)
- Sorry: Kho thot (kor-tot)
- Goodbye: La gon (la-gon)

Remember, Thai is a tonal language, so pay attention to the tones while pronouncing words. Practice these phrases with locals and don't be afraid to make mistakes. Thais appreciate your efforts to speak their language and will often help and encourage you along the way.

Learning Thai opens doors to deeper connections, cultural understanding, and a more enriching experience during your time in Thailand. Take the opportunity to learn this beautiful language and embrace the Thai way of life.

10.2: Making Friends and Building Relationships

Building meaningful relationships and making friends is an essential part of embracing the Thai lifestyle. Throughout my time in Thailand, I have had the pleasure of forming deep connections with Thai people, collaborating in music bands, and experiencing the warmth and hospitality they offer. Here are some insights and tips for making friends and fostering relationships in Thailand:

1. Thai Friends and Musical Connections: Over the years, I have formed numerous friendships with Thais, especially through my passion for music. Playing the saxophone in bands allowed me to connect with talented Thai musicians and share unforgettable musical experiences. Music has a way of bringing people together and transcending language barriers. Whether it's joining a band, attending music events, or exploring local music scenes, music can serve as a powerful platform for building relationships.

2. English Proficiency: It's worth noting that English proficiency in Thailand has been increasing, especially among the younger generation. Many Thais, particularly in urban areas and popular tourist destinations, have basic English language skills. This can facilitate communication and create opportunities for interaction with locals. However, learning some basic Thai phrases can still go

a long way in showing your genuine interest and respect for the local culture.

3. Cultural Exchange: Engaging in cultural exchange activities is an excellent way to meet people and make friends in Thailand. Participate in local festivals, attend temple events, or join community projects. These experiences not only allow you to immerse yourself in Thai traditions and customs but also provide opportunities to connect with locals who share similar interests.

4. Language Exchange: Language exchange is a two-way street where you can learn Thai while helping someone learn your native language. Join language exchange programs, online platforms, or attend language exchange meetups. This allows you to connect with Thai language learners who can become friends and provide insights into the local culture.

5. Join Clubs and Groups: Joining clubs or interest-based groups is a fantastic way to meet like-minded individuals in Thailand. Whether it's sports, hobbies, or volunteering, there are various clubs and organizations catering to different interests. By participating in these activities, you can connect with individuals who share common passions and develop friendships along the way.

6. Be Open and Respectful: Thai culture values politeness, respect, and harmony. Embrace these values in your interactions with locals. Show genuine interest in their culture, traditions, and way of life. Be open-minded, patient, and willing to learn from others. By demonstrating respect and cultural sensitivity, you can build strong and lasting relationships with Thai people.

Remember, building friendships takes time and effort, regardless of the country. Embrace the Thai lifestyle with an open heart and a willingness to connect with the local community. By engaging in activities, cultural exchange, and being respectful, you can create meaningful connections and form lasting friendships in Thailand. Enjoy the warmth and hospitality that Thai people have to offer, and cherish the enriching experiences that come with building relationships in this beautiful country.

10.3: Thai Cultural Etiquette in Social Settings

When embracing the Thai lifestyle, it's important to familiarize yourself with the cultural norms and etiquette that prevail in Thai society. Thai culture is known for its politeness, respect, and a certain level of conservatism. As I document my experiences on my YouTube channel, one aspect to note is that my wife is rarely physically affectionate with me on camera due to Thailand's conservative culture.

In Thai society, public displays of affection, such as kissing or hugging, are less common compared to some Western cultures. Thai people tend to prioritize personal space and boundaries, and it is customary to exercise restraint when it comes to physical contact, particularly in public or formal settings. This cultural difference is something that I've come to understand and respect throughout my time in Thailand.

It's essential to be mindful of cultural expectations and adjust our behavior accordingly. By respecting these cultural boundaries, we demonstrate our understanding and appreciation of Thai values. While every individual and situation may vary, it's advisable to be cautious and refrain from public acts of intimacy that may be considered inappropriate in the local context.

Understanding Thai greetings and the concept of the "wai" is another important aspect of Thai cultural etiquette. The wai is a traditional Thai greeting performed by pressing your palms together at chest level and slightly bowing your head. When greeting someone, it's customary for the younger or lower-ranking person to initiate the wai. The depth of the bow and the position of the hands may vary depending on the situation and the level of respect being shown.

Respecting elders and hierarchy is deeply ingrained in Thai culture. It is customary to address older individuals using appropriate honorifics and titles, such as "Pee" for an older sibling or "Khun" for someone older or of higher status. Demonstrating deference to those in positions of authority or seniority is an integral part of Thai social interactions.

Dressing modestly and respectfully is important, particularly when participating in social gatherings or visiting religious sites. Thai customs encourage wearing attire that covers the shoulders, chest, and knees. Revealing or provocative clothing may be considered inappropriate in certain settings, so it's best to err on the side of modesty.

Thai dining etiquette also has its unique customs. Waiting for the host or the eldest person to start eating before beginning your meal is customary. Using utensils such as spoons and forks is common practice, although some traditional dishes may be enjoyed with hands. It is also customary to remove your shoes before entering someone's home or a sacred place.

Lastly, exercising cultural sensitivity is vital when interacting with Thai people. Avoid making negative comments or criticizing aspects related to the Thai monarchy, religion, or cultural practices. Being mindful of your language, tone, and overall behavior when discussing sensitive topics will help foster positive connections and a deeper understanding of Thai culture.

By embracing Thai cultural etiquette in social settings, respecting personal boundaries, and being mindful of conservative values, we can effectively engage with Thai people and create meaningful relationships while immersing ourselves in the rich and diverse culture of Thailand.

10.4: Wellness and Mindfulness

Thailand offers a rich spiritual landscape that has greatly influenced my own personal growth and perspective. Living in this culturally diverse country has provided me with a deep appreciation for the spiritual practices found here. My own spiritual journey has been shaped by a blend of Hindu and Buddhist philosophies, which are prevalent throughout Thailand.

One aspect that has significantly contributed to my spiritual growth is the exposure to Buddhist teachings. Buddhism is deeply ingrained in Thai culture, and temples can be found in every corner of the country. These temples serve as places of worship, meditation, and spiritual contemplation. The serene and tranquil atmosphere within these temples allows for a profound sense of peace and mindfulness.

Additionally, my connection to the spiritual realm in Thailand has been strengthened through personal experiences and interactions with the local community. I have been fortunate to have a have met my wife's uncle, who was a high-ranking monk. Sadly, he recently passed away, but his wisdom and guidance continue to inspire me.

For those considering a move to Thailand, I believe there are immense spiritual benefits to be gained. The country's emphasis on mindfulness and spiritual practices provides a conducive environment for personal growth and self-discovery. Engaging in meditation, yoga, or other wellness practices can help foster a deeper connection with oneself and the world around us.

Moreover, Thailand's natural beauty, such as its lush forests, serene mountains, and tranquil beaches, offers a perfect backdrop for spiritual exploration and rejuvenation. Nature has a way of grounding us and reminding us of the interconnectedness of all living beings.

Whether it's through attending meditation retreats, participating in spiritual ceremonies, or simply embracing the Thai way of life, immersing oneself in the rich spiritual heritage of Thailand can be a transformative experience. The country's spiritual essence has the potential to ignite a greater sense of purpose, inner peace, and mindfulness in one's daily life.

It is important to approach these spiritual practices with an open heart and mind, respecting the cultural traditions and beliefs of the local people. Engaging with the local community, seeking guidance from knowledgeable practitioners, and participating in ceremonies and rituals can offer a deeper understanding of Thai spirituality.

Living in a village with strong Khmer influences, I have also been exposed to unique regional beliefs and practices that add an intriguing dimension to my spiritual journey. It is important to note that these beliefs are specific to our village and may not be widely known or practiced throughout Thailand.

In addition to the dominant Buddhist and Hindu philosophies, our village has a rich history of Khmer spiritual traditions. The Khmer people, who migrated to the region centuries ago, brought with them their own set of beliefs and rituals. These practices often revolve around the veneration of ancestral spirits, the worship of local deities, and the observation of auspicious days and rituals.

Furthermore, our village also has pockets of individuals who are engaged in practices related to witchcraft and black magic, which are not widely acknowledged or understood by the general public. These lesser-known transitions involve the use of spells, charms, and rituals to influence or manipulate certain aspects of life. While these practices may be shrouded in mystery and controversy, they are part of the fabric of our local culture and belief system.

Living amidst these unique regional beliefs has provided me with a broader perspective on spirituality and the interconnectedness of various faiths and practices. It has taught me to appreciate the diversity of human beliefs and to approach them with respect and an open mind. Witnessing the different spiritual expressions in our village has deepened my understanding of the human quest for meaning and connection.

It is worth noting that these regional beliefs and practices are not widely promoted or accessible to outsiders. They are deeply rooted in the local community and require a level of trust and understanding to be shared. As an outsider, it is important to approach these practices with sensitivity, respect, and a willingness to learn from those who hold these beliefs.

11. OVERCOMING LANGUAGE AND CULTURAL BARRIERS

11.1: Overcoming Language and Cultural Barriers

Moving to a new country like Thailand comes with its fair share of challenges, particularly when it comes to language and cultural differences. As an expat, I understand the initial struggles of adapting to a new language and navigating cultural norms. However, with a proactive mindset and a willingness to learn, you can overcome these barriers and embrace your new life in Thailand.

One of the key challenges is the Thai language, which may seem daunting at first. I, too, faced difficulties when I first arrived in Thailand. However, I found that immersing myself in the language was the most effective way to overcome this hurdle. Surrounding yourself with locals and practicing Thai conversations can greatly enhance your language skills. Additionally, there are language schools and online resources available that offer Thai language courses tailored to expats. Taking these courses can significantly improve your ability to communicate and connect with the local community.

Understanding and adapting to Thai cultural norms is equally important. Thai culture has its own unique customs and traditions that may differ from what you're accustomed to. It's essential to approach these differences with an open mind and a willingness to learn. Observing and respecting local customs can help you build meaningful relationships and integrate into the community.

To overcome cultural barriers, consider immersing yourself in Thai culture. Engage in local activities, attend festivals, and explore the diverse cuisine. By participating in these experiences, you not only gain a deeper understanding of Thai culture but also create opportunities to connect with locals and build friendships.

Additionally, seeking guidance from expat communities and support groups can be invaluable. These communities often consist of individuals who have already navigated the challenges of living in Thailand and can provide advice, support, and a sense of belonging. Online forums, social media groups, and local expat organizations are excellent resources to connect with like-minded individuals and seek guidance on various aspects of living in Thailand.

Embracing patience and having a sense of humor can also go a long way in overcoming language and cultural barriers. Recognize that misunderstandings may happen, and it's okay to make mistakes along the way. Thai people are generally welcoming and understanding, and they appreciate sincere efforts to learn their language and culture.

Remember, overcoming language and cultural barriers is a gradual process. Embrace the journey of learning, stay open-minded, and be proactive in seeking opportunities to immerse yourself in the Thai language and culture. With time, patience, and a genuine curiosity to understand and connect with the local community, you will find yourself adapting and thriving in your new life in Thailand.

11.2: Dealing with Homesickness and Culture Shock

Moving to a new country like Thailand can be an exciting and transformative experience, but it's not uncommon to experience bouts of homesickness and culture shock along the way. Whether you're missing your family, friends, or the familiarity of your home country, it's important to acknowledge and address these feelings. In this section, we'll explore strategies for coping with homesickness and culture shock, as well as how to navigate the transition to a new culture.

Homesickness is a natural response to being away from familiar surroundings and loved ones. It's perfectly normal to miss your family, friends, and the comforts of home. However, there are several techniques that can help alleviate homesickness and make your adjustment to life in Thailand more manageable.

Firstly, maintaining regular communication with your loved ones back home can provide a sense of connection and support. Thanks to modern technology, staying in touch has become easier than ever. Schedule regular video calls, exchange messages, and share updates with your family and friends. Knowing that you have their support and understanding can greatly ease feelings of homesickness.

Creating a sense of home in your new environment is another effective strategy. Surround yourself with familiar objects or mementos that hold sentimental value. Decorate your living space with items that remind you of home, such as photographs, artwork, or souvenirs. Establishing a comforting and familiar space can help alleviate homesickness and make your new surroundings feel more like home.

Engaging in activities that bring you joy and fulfillment is crucial for combating homesickness. Pursue your hobbies, explore your interests, and seek out new experiences in Thailand. Engaging in meaningful activities not only distracts from feelings of homesickness but also provides opportunities to meet new people and build a support network.

Culture shock, on the other hand, is the disorienting feeling that arises from encountering unfamiliar customs, values, and ways of life. It's common to experience a sense of confusion or even frustration when adapting to a new culture. However, with time and effort, you can navigate culture shock and develop a deeper understanding and appreciation for Thai culture.

One of the most effective ways to overcome culture shock is to immerse yourself in the local culture. Embrace the customs, traditions, and cuisine of Thailand. Engage in cultural activities, attend festivals, and explore the vibrant local markets. By actively participating in the cultural fabric of Thailand, you'll gain a deeper understanding of its people and their way of life.

Seeking out local friendships and connections can also help alleviate culture shock. Engaging with Thai locals not only provides insights into their culture but also helps build a support network. Join language exchange programs, volunteer in local organizations, or participate in community events. These activities provide opportunities to interact with locals, learn from them, and form meaningful connections.

Developing a curious and open mindset is essential for navigating culture shock. Embrace the differences and approach them as opportunities for personal growth and learning. Challenge your assumptions and preconceived notions, and be willing to adapt and adjust your perspectives. Learning about Thai customs, traditions, and social etiquette can go a long way in easing culture shock and building cultural competence.

It's worth noting that over time, as you become more integrated into Thai culture, you may experience reverse culture shock when returning to your home country. This is a common phenomenon where you feel a sense of disorientation and unease when confronted with the cultural norms and expectations of your home country. To mitigate this, maintain connections with fellow expats, continue engaging with Thai culture even while abroad, and consider having your family visit you in Thailand. By creating a balance between your Thai and home cultures, you can better manage the effects of reverse culture shock.

Additionally, as you settle into your new life in Thailand, you may find yourself drawn to sharing your experiences and insights with others who are considering a similar journey. Consulting and guiding individuals who are interested in moving to Thailand or starting a YouTube channel can be a fulfilling way to contribute your knowledge and help others navigate their own paths. Your firsthand experiences and understanding of the challenges and rewards of living in Thailand can be invaluable to those seeking guidance.

By following these strategies and maintaining a positive outlook, you can navigate the challenges of homesickness and culture shock, and fully embrace the rich and vibrant lifestyle that Thailand has to offer.

11.3: Coping with Climate and Weather Changes

M oving to a new country often means adapting to a different climate, and Thailand is no exception. The climate in Thailand can vary significantly depending on the region, and it's important to be prepared for the weather changes you may encounter. In this section, we'll discuss coping with climate and weather changes, drawing from personal experiences and practical tips.

One of the significant climate challenges in Thailand is the hot season, which can be intense and sweltering. In my early years on the farm, I didn't have air conditioning, and I had to acclimate to the heat and humidity. It was a process that took time, but eventually, I adjusted to the climate. However, I still find the hot season to be challenging, especially when it comes to outdoor activities like working in the garden. The scorching heat can be relentless, and it's important to take precautions to stay cool and hydrated during this time.

To cope with the hot season and other weather changes, it's crucial to find ways to stay comfortable and engaged. Here are some tips to help you navigate the climate challenges in Thailand:

1. Stay Hydrated: Drink plenty of water throughout the day, especially during the hot season. Carry a reusable water bottle with you wherever you go and make sure to replenish your fluids regularly.

2. Seek Shade and Cool Spaces: When the sun is at its peak, try to stay in shaded areas or air-conditioned environments. This can provide relief from the intense heat and help you avoid exhaustion.

3. Dress Appropriately: Wear light and breathable clothing made from natural fabrics like cotton to stay cool. Opt for loose-fitting

outfits that allow air circulation.

4. Plan Activities Wisely: During the hot season, plan your outdoor activities for early mornings or evenings when the temperature is relatively cooler. This way, you can still enjoy outdoor pursuits without feeling overwhelmed by the heat.

5. Explore Indoor Entertainment: If the weather conditions make it challenging to engage in outdoor activities, consider exploring indoor entertainment options. Thailand offers a diverse range of attractions, including museums, art galleries, and shopping malls, where you can enjoy air-conditioned spaces and cultural experiences.

6. Find Indoor Hobbies: Use the hot season as an opportunity to discover new indoor hobbies or pursue existing interests. Engage in activities like reading, writing, painting, or learning a new skill. This can help you stay productive and entertained while avoiding the discomfort of the outdoor heat.

It's important to note that climate preferences and tolerance levels vary from person to person. While some individuals may acclimate quickly to the Thai weather, others may find certain seasons more challenging. Remember to listen to your body and adjust your activities and routines accordingly.

As you adapt to the climate changes, it's also worth exploring the diverse beauty and attractions that Thailand offers throughout the year. From stunning waterfalls and lush national parks to cultural festivals and culinary delights, there's always something to discover regardless of the weather.

12. FINDING LOVE IN THAILAND

Finding Love in the Land of Smiles

When people think of Thailand, the first things that come to mind are often the stunning beaches, rich cultural heritage, and warm hospitality. However, for many, Thailand also holds the promise of finding love and building meaningful relationships. In this chapter, we will explore the different avenues and experiences of finding love in Thailand, offering insights, stories, and practical advice to navigate this unique journey.

1. The Allure of Love in Thailand

Thailand has long been a magnet for individuals seeking love, romance, and companionship. The country's vibrant culture, exotic beauty, and welcoming nature create an environment conducive to forming connections. Many people are drawn to Thailand's charm, hoping to find a partner who shares their sense of adventure and embraces the Thai way of life.

2. My Personal Journey

Allow me to share my own story of how I met my wife in Thailand. It all started online, as we connected through a shared passion for volunteering with elephants. Little did I know that this virtual connection would blossom into a profound and loving relationship. As we met in person, I discovered that my wife was shy, and it took months of hand-holding and patient courtship before our first kiss. Our journey together has been filled with adventure, love, and mutual growth.

3. Exploring Different Avenues

When it comes to finding love in Thailand, there are various avenues to explore. While some may associate Thailand with its infamous bar scene, it's essential to approach the topic with sensitivity and without judgment. Bar girls and escorts play a role in the nightlife industry, but it's crucial to recognize that they are individuals with their own stories and aspirations. For those seeking genuine connections, there are numerous other avenues to explore.

4. Meeting Professionals and Like-Minded Individuals

Thailand is home to a diverse and talented workforce, including doctors, teachers, and professionals in various fields. Many of these individuals, driven by their careers and commitments, may not have ample time to socialize or engage in the party scene. This opens up opportunities for meaningful connections beyond the nightlife. Online platforms, social events, and community gatherings can provide avenues to meet these working professionals, who are often looking for genuine relationships.

5. Pitfalls and Challenges

While Thailand offers a wealth of opportunities for finding love, it's essential to navigate potential pitfalls and challenges along the way. Language and cultural barriers can present initial hurdles, but with patience and a willingness to learn, these obstacles can be overcome. Building trust and understanding is crucial, especially when financial matters come into play. It is advisable to know someone well before entering into any financial exchanges, as scams and misunderstandings can occur.

6. Maximizing Your Chances

To increase your chances of finding love in Thailand, consider the following tips:

- Embrace the Thai culture: Show genuine interest in Thai customs, traditions, and beliefs. This will not only enrich your understanding of the local culture but also demonstrate your openness and willingness to connect on a deeper level.

- Learn the language: While many Thais speak basic English, making an effort to learn Thai can go a long way in building connections and bridging cultural gaps. Immersion programs, language classes, and language exchange platforms can help you grasp the basics and communicate with locals more effectively.

- Engage in community activities: Participate in local festivals, volunteer initiatives, or community projects. These activities provide opportunities to meet like-minded individuals and develop connections based on shared interests and values.

- Stay open-minded: Thailand is a diverse country with people from various backgrounds and walks of life. Stay open-minded and embrace the diversity you encounter. Be willing to step out of your comfort zone and engage with people from different walks of life, as you never know where you might find a deep connection.

- Online dating platforms: In the digital age, online dating has become increasingly popular and can be an effective way to meet potential partners. There are reputable dating platforms specifically catering to individuals interested in dating in Thailand. Exercise caution, take the time to get to know someone before meeting in person, and prioritize safety.

- Socialize in expat communities: Expats living in Thailand

often form tight-knit communities. Engaging in social events, attending meetups, or joining clubs and interest groups can help you connect with fellow expats who may share similar experiences and perspectives.

- Seek local recommendations: Local Thai friends or acquaintances can be invaluable resources when it comes to finding love in Thailand. They can provide insights, introduce you to their social circles, and offer advice on cultural norms and expectations.

7. Respecting Thai Cultural Etiquette

Thai cultural norms place great importance on respect, politeness, and modesty. Public displays of affection, particularly intimate physical contact, are generally frowned upon. Understanding and adhering to these cultural norms show respect for the Thai way of life and can help foster positive relationships.

8. Embracing Love in a Changing World

As the world continues to evolve, so does the landscape of finding love in Thailand. The rise of technology and increased connectivity has transformed how people meet and connect. However, it's essential to balance the convenience of online interactions with the importance of genuine connections and getting to know someone beyond superficial impressions.

9. Love Beyond Borders

Thailand's allure goes beyond its borders, attracting individuals from around the globe who seek love and companionship. The multicultural fabric of Thailand offers opportunities for cross-cultural relationships, enriching experiences, and mutual growth. Embrace the beauty of diverse love stories and the possibilities that arise when different cultures intertwine.

In the realm of love, there are stories of heartbreak and

disillusionment that can leave individuals feeling jaded. Some people have experienced unfortunate situations where their possessions were taken, or they fell victim to scams or manipulative tactics. While these stories exist, it's essential not to let them overshadow the beauty and potential of love in Thailand.

It's important to approach relationships with an open heart and a level-headed mindset. It's easy to become jaded by what we read or hear online about Thailand and its people. However, it's crucial to remember that generalizations and negative experiences do not define an entire country or its population.

Instead of harboring bitterness, focus on the reset that Thailand offers. Use these experiences as lessons and opportunities for growth. Understand that every culture has its complexities and challenges, and Thailand is no exception. By approaching relationships with caution, cultural sensitivity, and a willingness to learn, you can pave the way for positive and fulfilling connections.

One way to avoid bitterness is by fostering a supportive community. Engage with other expats and locals who have found love and built successful relationships in Thailand. Share experiences, seek advice, and learn from those who have navigated the terrain before you. Surrounding yourself with positive influences can help you maintain a healthy perspective and restore your faith in love.

Another vital aspect is self-reflection. Take the time to assess your own expectations, values, and boundaries. Understand that cultural differences may shape the dynamics of relationships in Thailand, and being aware of these nuances can help you navigate them more effectively. By understanding yourself better, you can communicate your needs and desires clearly, setting the foundation for healthier connections.

Lastly, remember that no relationship is immune to challenges. Love requires effort, understanding, and compromise regardless of where you are in the world. Embrace the journey as an opportunity for personal growth and cultural exchange. Celebrate the diversity that Thailand brings and appreciate the unique experiences that unfold along the way.

While some individuals have had unfortunate experiences in love in Thailand, it's important not to let these stories overshadow the potential for beautiful connections. By avoiding bitterness, fostering a supportive community, engaging in self-reflection, and embracing the reset that Thailand offers, you can approach relationships with a renewed sense of hope and openness. Remember, love knows no boundaries, and Thailand's rich cultural tapestry has the potential to weave beautiful stories of love and companionship.

In conclusion, finding love in Thailand can be an exciting and rewarding journey, filled with unique experiences and profound connections. Whether you meet someone online, through community engagement, or by chance encounter, be open to the possibilities and approach your search for love with patience, respect, and genuine intent. Thailand's cultural richness and warm-hearted people offer a fertile ground for love to blossom. So, immerse yourself in the Thai experience, embrace the opportunities, and let love find its way into your life.

CONCLUSION

Embracing Thailand's
Vibrant Expat Journey

As we reach the end of this journey, and the beginning of yours, I am reminded of the countless stories and experiences shared throughout our exploration of moving to Thailand as an expat. From the initial allure and intrigue to the realities and challenges, we have delved deep into the nuances of life in the Land of Smiles. It is my hope that this book has served as a guiding light, offering practical advice, personal anecdotes, and a glimpse into the diverse tapestry that Thailand weaves.

Moving to Thailand as an expat is a transformative experience. It opens the doors to a world of adventure, cultural immersion, and self-discovery. The decision to uproot one's life and embrace a new land is not without its trials, but the rewards are immeasurable. Throughout these chapters, we have explored the intricacies of Thai culture, the allure of pristine beaches and tranquil villages, the challenges of language and adaptation, the pursuit of love, and the endless possibilities for personal growth and fulfillment.

In recounting my own experiences and those shared by fellow expats, we have painted a vivid picture of life in Thailand. From the bustling streets of Bangkok to the serene rural landscapes, each corner of this country holds a unique charm. The warmth and hospitality of the Thai people have touched our lives, reminding us that even in the face of challenges, we can find solace and support in this vibrant community.

As you embark on your own expat journey to Thailand, I encourage you to approach it with an open mind and a sense of adventure. Embrace the cultural diversity, savor the tantalizing flavors of Thai cuisine, and immerse yourself in the traditions and festivals that bring this nation to life. Seek out connections with both locals and fellow expats, for it is through these relationships that we find the true essence of Thailand.

Remember, this book is merely a guide, a stepping stone on your path. Your experiences will be uniquely yours, and the memories you create will shape the narrative of your own expat adventure. Cherish the ups and downs, celebrate the victories, and learn from the challenges. Thailand has a way of captivating our hearts and transforming us in unexpected ways.

Whether you find yourself teaching English in bustling city schools, starting a business in the tranquil countryside, or embarking on a personal quest for love and connection, Thailand welcomes you with open arms. It is a land of contrasts, where ancient traditions merge with modernity, and where the past and present intertwine harmoniously.

As you turn the final page of this book, remember that the true essence of Thailand lies not in its breathtaking landscapes or bustling markets, but in the connections we forge and the moments we share with its people. May your expat journey be filled with joy, growth, and a profound sense of belonging. Thailand awaits you with open arms, ready to embrace you as one of its own.

Sawasdee krub (greetings) and farewell, fellow expat. May your new chapter in Thailand be filled with endless adventures and meaningful connections.

ABOUT THE AUTHOR

Ryan, also known by his online moniker Ryan Otis, is a passionate explorer and storyteller with a deep connection to Thailand. Alongside his beloved family, including his two sons Otis and Hugo and his wife Damo, Ryan has carved out a fulfilling life on a quaint farm in rural Thailand. This idyllic setting not only allows them to embrace sustainable practices but, more importantly, to cherish their time together as a close-knit family.

With a keen interest in capturing the essence of rural Thailand, Ryan and his family have embarked on a captivating YouTube journey, documenting the rich cultural tapestry that thrives in their local community. Through their videos, they offer a unique perspective on the authentic Thai way of life, sharing stories of resilience, traditions, and the beauty of simplicity.

As an experienced expat who has navigated the challenges and joys of moving to Thailand, Ryan offers personalized consultations to those seeking guidance on their own Thai adventure. Whether you're contemplating a move to this captivating country or considering starting a YouTube channel to share your own experiences, Ryan is ready to lend his expertise and support. You can reach him directly via email at thenakedguruexperience@gmail.com or see him and his family on the youtube channel: Life In Bamboo.

Ryan's commitment to authenticity, cultural immersion, and sustainable living shines through his work and personal experiences. He understands the intricate nuances of Thai culture and the complexities of adapting to a new way of life. With his genuine passion for sharing knowledge and fostering connections, Ryan is dedicated to helping others embark on their own transformative journeys in Thailand.

Through his words, videos, and consultations, Ryan invites you to embrace the vibrant and diverse landscape of Thailand, to immerse yourself in its traditions, and to create a life filled with meaningful connections and unforgettable experiences.

Printed by Amazon Italia Logistica S.r.l.
Torrazza Piemonte (TO), Italy

58911250R00077